Dedication

To all those who ever struggled with learning a
foreign language and to Wolfgang Karfunkel

Also by Yatir Nitzany

Conversational German Quick and Easy

....

Conversational Dutch Quick and Easy

....

Conversational Norwegian Quick and Easy

....

Conversational Russian Quick and Easy

....

Conversational Ukranian Quick and Easy

....

Conversational Polish Quick and Easy

....

Conversational Bulgarian Quick and Easy

....

Conversational Yiddish Quick and Easy

....

Conversational Armenian Quick and Easy

....

Conversational Hebrew Quick and Easy

....

Conversational Arabic Quick and Easy
Classical Arabic

....

Conversational Arabic Quick and Easy
Lebanese Arabic

....

Conversational Arabic Quick and Easy
Egyptian

....

Conversational Arabic Quick and Easy
Moroccan Dialect

....

Conversational Arabic Quick and Easy
Emirati Dialect

....

Conversational Arabic Quick and Easy
Iraqi Dialect

Conversational Languages Quick and Easy

THE SPANISH, FRENCH, ITALIAN, AND PORUTGUESE LANGUAGE

YATIR NITZANY

Foreword

About Myself

For many years I struggled to learn Spanish, and I still knew no more than about twenty words. Consequently, I was extremely frustrated. One day I stumbled upon this method as I was playing around with word combinations. Suddenly, I came to the realization that every language has a certain core group of words that are most commonly used and, simply by learning them, one could gain the ability to engage in quick and easy conversational Spanish.

I discovered which words those were, and I narrowed them down to three hundred and fifty that, once memorized, one could connect and create one's own sentences. The variations were and are *infinite*! By using this incredibly simple technique, I could converse at a proficient level and speak Spanish. Within a week, I astonished my Spanish-speaking friends with my newfound ability. The next semester I registered at my university for a Spanish language course, and I applied the same principles I had learned in that class (grammar, additional vocabulary, future and past tense, etc.) to those three hundred and fifty words I already had memorized, and immediately I felt as if I had grown wings and learned how to fly.

At the end of the semester, we took a class trip to San José, Costa Rica. I was like a fish in water, while the rest of my classmates were floundering and still struggling to converse. Throughout the following months, I again applied the same principle to other languages—French, Portuguese, Italian, and Arabic, all of which I now speak proficiently, thanks to this very simple technique.

This method is by far the fastest way to master quick and easy conversational language skills. There is no other technique that compares to my concept. It is effective, it worked for me, and it will work for you. Be consistent with my program, and you too will succeed the way I and many, many others have.

Contents

INTRODUCTION TO
THE PROGRAM

People often dream about learning a foreign language, but usually they never do it. Some feel that they just won't be able to do it while others believe that they don't have the time. Whatever your reason is, it's time to set that aside. With my new method, you will have enough time, and you will not fail. You will actually learn how to speak the fundamentals of the language—fluently in as little as a few days. Of course, you won't speak perfect Spanish, French, Italian, or Portuguese at first, but you will certainly gain significant proficiency. For example, if you travel to Europe or South America, you will almost effortlessly be able engage in basic conversational communication with the locals in the present tense and you will no longer be intimidated by culture shock. It's time to relax. Learning a language is a valuable skill that connects people of multiple cultures around the world— and you now have the tools to join them.

How does my method work? I have taken twenty-seven of the most commonly used languages in the world and distilled from them the three hundred and fifty most frequently used words in any language. This process took three years of observation and research, and during that time, I determined which words I felt were most important for this method of basic conversational communication. In that time, I chose these words in such a way that they were structurally interrelated and that, when combined, form sentences. Thus, once you succeed in memorizing these words, you will be able to combine these words and form your own sentences. The words are spread over twenty pages. In fact, there are just nine basic words that will effectively build bridges, enabling you to speak in an understandable manner (please see Building Bridges at the end of every section). The words will also combine easily in sentences, for example, enabling you to ask simple questions, make basic statements, and obtain a rudimentary understanding of others' communications. I have also created Memorization-Made-Easy Techniques for this program in order to help with the memorization of the vocabulary Please see Reading and Pronunciation at the end of each section in order to gain proficiency in the reading and pronunciation of the language prior to starting this program.

My book is mainly intended for basic present tense vocal communication, meaning anyone can easily use it to "get by" linguistically while visiting a foreign country without learning the entire language. With practice, you will be 100 percent understandable to native speakers, which is your aim. One disclaimer: this is not a grammar book, though it does address minute and essential grammar rules. Therefore, understanding complex sentences with obscure words in the language is beyond the scope of this book.

People who have tried this method have been successful, and by the time you finish this book, you will understand and be understood in basic conversational language. This is the best basis to learn not only the these four languages but any language. This is an entirely revolutionary, no-fail concept, and your ability to combine the pieces of the "language puzzle" together will come with great ease, especially if you use this program prior to beginning a language class.

This is the best program that was ever designed to teach the reader how to become conversational. Other conversational programs will only teach you phrases. But this is the only program that will teach you how to create your own sentences for the purpose of becoming conversational.

Conversational
Spanish
Quick and Easy

THE MOST INNOVATIVE AND REVOLUTIONARY
TECHNIQUE TO MASTER CONVERSATIONAL SPANISH

YATIR NITZANY

THE SPANISH LANGUAGE

Spanish originated in Spain, and it closely resembles Portuguese, as both are Latin in their derivation and, therefore, Romance languages. The Spanish language was spread during the 1500s by Spanish colonialists coming from Spain to South America. Since then, the language has grown and is now the fourth most-spoken language in the world. Spanish is still rising in popularity, as it has 98 million non-native speakers and 402 million native speakers. Don't you want to be a member of the ever-growing population of Spanish speakers? Now you can be, if you follow the simple instructions of this program.

Spoken in: Spain, South America, Mexico, and the Caribbean

MEMORIZATION MADE EASY

There is no doubt the three hundred and fifty words in my program are the required essentials in order to engage in quick and easy basic conversation in any foreign language. However, some people may experience difficulty in the memorization. For this reason, I created Memorization Made Easy. This memorization technique will make this program so simple and fun that it's unbelievable! I have spread the words over the following twenty pages. Each page contains a vocabulary table of ten to fifteen words. Below every vocabulary box, sentences are composed from the words on the page that you have just studied. This aids greatly in memorization. Once you succeed in memorizing the first page, then proceed to the second page. Upon completion of the second page, go back to the first and review. Then proceed to the third page. After memorizing the third, go back to the first and second and repeat. And so on. As you continue, begin to combine words and create your own sentences in your head. Every time you proceed to the following page, you will notice words from the previous pages will be present in those simple sentences as well, because repetition is one of the most crucial aspects in learning any foreign language. Upon completion of your twenty pages, congratulations, you have absorbed the required words and gained a basic, quick-and-easy proficiency and you should now be able to create your own sentences and say anything you wish in Spanish. This is a crash course in conversational Spanish, and it works!

For further assistance in the memorization of the vocabulary of this program, you may also purchase the audio version of this book, which is featured on Audible, iTunes, and Amazon.

NOTE TO THE READER

The purpose of this book is merely to enable you to communicate in Spanish. In the program itself (pages 16-41), you may notice that the composition of some of those sentences might sound rather clumsy. This is intentional. These sentences were formulated in a specific way to serve two purposes: to facilitate the easy memorization of the vocabulary and to teach you how to combine the words in order to form your own sentences for quick and easy communication, rather than making complete literal sense in the English language. So keep in mind that this is not a phrase book!

As the title suggests, the sole purpose of this program is for conversational use only. It is based on the mirror translation technique. These sentences, as well as the translations are not incorrect, just a little clumsy. Latin languages, Semitic languages, and Anglo-Germanic languages, as well as a few others, are compatible with the mirror translation technique.

Many users say that this method surpasses any other known language learning technique that is currently out there on the market. Just stick with the program and you will achieve wonders!

Again, I wish to stress this program is by no means, shape, or form a phrase book! The sole purpose of this book is to give you a fundamental platform to enable you to connect certain words to become conversational. Please also read the "Introduction" and the "About Me" section prior to commencing the program.

In order to succeed with my method, please start on the very first page of the program and fully master one page at a time prior to proceeding to the next. Otherwise, you will overwhelm yourself and fail. Please do not skip pages, nor start from the middle of the book.

It is a myth that certain people are born with the talent to learn a language, and this book disproves that myth. With this method, anyone can learn a foreign language as long as he or she follows these explicit directions:

* Memorize the vocabulary on each page.

* Follow that memorization by using a notecard to cover the words you have just memorized and test yourself.

* Then read the sentences following that are created from the vocabulary bank that you just mastered.

* Once fully memorized, give yourself the green light to proceed to the next page.

Again, if you proceed to the following page without mastering the previous, you are guaranteed to gain nothing from this book. If you follow the prescribed steps, you will realize just how effective and simplistic this method is.

THE PROGRAM

Let's Begin! "Vocabulary"
(Memorize the Vocabulary)

I	Yo
With you	Contigo
With him / with her	Con él / Con ella
With us	Con Nosotros
For you	Para Ti
Without him	Sin él
Without them	(masculine)Sin Ellos / (fem)Sin Ellas
Always	Siempre
Was	Estuvo
This	Este, Esta, esto
Is	Es / Esta
Sometimes	Algunas Veces
Maybe	Tal Vez /Quizás
Are you	Tu eres / Estas
Better	Mejor
I am	Yo Soy / Estoy
He / She, her	Él / Ella
From	De

Sentences composed from the vocabulary (now you can speak the sentences and combine the words).

I am with you

Estoy Contigo

Sometimes I am with him

Algunas veces estoy con él

Are you without them today?

¿Estás sin ellos hoy?

Sometimes you are with us at the mall

Algunas veces estás con nosotros en el mall.

This is for you

Esto es para ti

I am always with her

Estoy siempre con ella

I am from Canada

Yo soy de Canadá

Are you from Canada?

Tú eres de Canadá?

Concerning yo soy, estoy / es, esta & tu eres, estas, please refer to the permanent and temporary section on page 44.

I was	Estuve
To be	Estar / Ser
The	El / La / Los / Las
Same	Mismo / Igual
Good	Bueno
Here	Aquí
It's	Es / Esta
And	y (pronounced as *ie*)
Between	Entre
Now	Ahora
Later / After	Luego /Despues /Más tarde
If	Si
Yes	Sí
Then	Entonces
Tomorrow	Mañana
You	(*informal*)Tú/ (*formal*)usted
Also / too / as well	También

Between now and later
Entre ahora y luego
If it's later, then it's better tomorrow
Si es más tarde, entonces es mejor mañana.
This is good as well
Esto es bueno también
To be the same
Ser el mismo
Yes, you are very good
Sí, eres muy bueno
I was here with them
Yo estuve aquí con ellos
You and I
Tú y yo
The same day
El mismo día

*For pronunciation of ñ, please refer to Reading and Pronunciation, page 49.
*Concerning *estar* and *ser*, please refer to the Permanent and Temporary section, page 44.
*Concerning *el, la, los,* and *las*, please refer to the Singular and Plural section, page 43.
*Too is *también*. However, "too much" is *demasiado*. "I am too tired" / *estoy demasiado cansado.*
*In Spanish, the plural form of "you", regardless of whether formal or informal, is *ustedes*.

Me	Me
Ok	Ok / bien / bueno
Even if	Incluso
Afterwards	Luego
Worse	Peor
Where	Dónde
Everything	Todo
Somewhere	Algun Lugar
What	Qué
Almost	Casi
There	Allí

Afterwards is worse
Luego es peor
Even if I go now
Incluso si yo voy ahora
Where is everything?
¿Dónde está todo?
Maybe somewhere
Tal vez en algún lugar
What? I am almost there
¿Qué? Estoy casi allí
Where are you?
¿Dónde estás?

*For pronunciation of the *ll* in *allí*, please refer to page 49.
*In Spanish, the pronouns *me, mi,* and *mí* could be quite confusing. *Me* signifies "myself" and is accompanied with direct and indirect objects as will as with reflexive verbs. *Mi* means "my." *Mí,* signifying "me," is used for the purpose of prepositions.
*Direct object—*El me habló*
*Indirect object—*Ella me dijo*
*Reflexive verb—*Yo me llamo*
*Adjective—*Es mi primo*
*Object of preposition— *Esta casa es para mí*

House / Home	Casa / Hogar
In	En
Car	Auto / Carro
Already	Ya
Good morning	Buenos Días
How are you?	Cómo estas?
Where are you from?	De dondé eres?
Today	Hoy
Hello	Hola
What is your name?	¿Cómo te llamas?
How old are you?	Cuantos años tienes?
Son	Hijo
Daughter	Hija
At	En el / En la
Very	Muy
Hard	Difícil / Duro
Without us	Sin nosotros

She is without a car, so maybe she is still at the house?
¿Ella está sin auto, entonces quizás ella está todavía en la casa?
I am in the car already with your son and your daughter
Ya estoy en el auto con tu hijo y tu hija
Good morning, how are you today?
¿Buenos días, cómo estás hoy?
Hello, what is your name?
Hola, cómo te llamas?
How old are you?
¿Cuántos años tienes?
This is very hard, but it's not impossible
Éste es muy difícil, pero no es imposible
Where are you from?
¿De dónde eres?

*In Spanish, the phrase "it's not" is flipped around—no es or no esta.
*"How old are you?," cuantos años tienes, literally means "how many years do you have?"

*"Please refer to page 49 for pronunciation of j in hija
*"What is your name" is ¿Cómo te llamas? however you can also say
¿Cuál es su nombre? translates to "which is your name."

Thank you	Gracias
For / In order to	Para *(or)* por
Anything	Cualquier cosa
It's	Es
Time	Tiempo
But	Pero
No / Not	No
I am not	Yo no estoy / Yo no soy
Away	Lejos / Distante
That	(M) Ese, (F) Esa
Similar	Similar
Other / Another	Otro
Side	Lado
Until	Hasta
Yesterday	Ayer
Still	Todavia
Since	Desde / Hace
Day	Día
Before	Antes

Thanks for anything
Gracias por cualquier cosa
It's almost time
Es casi tiempo
I am not here, I am away
No estoy aquí, estoy distante/lejos.
That is a similar house
Esa es una casa similar
I am from the other side
Soy del otro lado
But I was here until late yesterday
Pero estuve aquí hasta tarde ayer.
Since the other day
Desde el otro día

*In Spanish, the definition of *de* is "of" or "from." However, in the event that the article "the" follows "of" or "from" (*de*) (for example, "from the" or "of the"), the *de* + *el* merges into *del*. This case applies solely to the masculine article *el*. If *de* is followed by the feminine article *la*, you can't say *del*, only *de la*. The same applies with plurals (i.e., *las flores del jardin, las flores de los jardines, la maestra de la escuela, el maestro del colegio, el maestro de los colegios,* etc.).

However, when someone says, *Ella es del Canada* or *Juan es del Peru,* many people would simply say, *Ella es de Canada* or *Ella es de Peru.* The *del* is used only because the names of these countries are also *El Canada* and *El Peru.* There a few others such as *El Congo,* etc. You can also use the merging of *de* + *el* in a sentence such as *la enfermera del hospital central.*

I say / I am saying	Yo Digo / Estoy Diciendo
What time is it?	Qué Hora es?
I want	Quiero
Without you	Sin Ti
Everywhere	Todo Lugar / cada lugar / todas partes
I go / I am going	Yo voy (or) me voy
With	Con
My	(Singular)Mi / (Plural)Mis
Cousin	Primo
I need	Necesito
Right now	En este momento
Night	Noche
To see	Ver
Light	Luz
Outside	Afuera
That is	Eso es
Any	Cualquier
I see / I am seeing	Yo veo (or) soy/estoy viendo

I am saying no / I say no
Estoy diciendo no / Yo digo no
I want to see this during the day
Yo quiero ver esto durante el día
I see this everywhere
Veo esto en todas partes
I am happy without any of my cousins here
Estoy feliz sin cualquier de mis primos aquí.
I need to be there at night
Necesito estar allí en la noche
I see light outside
Yo veo luz afuera
What time is it right now?
¿Qué hora es en este momento?

*In Spanish, placing the pronoun "I" (yo) before a conjugated verb isn't required. For example, I want to use this is quiero usar esto instead of yo quiero usar esto. Although saying **yo** quiero usar isn't incorrect. The same rule also applies for the pronouns you, he, she, them, we. Read page 45 to learn more.
*This isn't a phrase book! The purpose of this book is solely to provide you with the tools to create your own sentences!

Place	Lugar
Easy	Fácil
To find	Encontrar
To look for/to search	Buscar
Near	Cerca / Acerca
To wait	Esperar
To sell	Vender
To use	Usar
To know	Saber
To decide	Decidir
Between	Entre
Both	Ambos / Dos
To	A/ al / a la

This place is easy to find
Este lugar es muy fácil de encontrar
I need to look for you next to the car
Yo necesito buscar para ti cerca del auto.
I am saying to wait until tomorrow
Yo digo esperar hasta mañana.
It's easy to sell this table
Está fácil vender esta mesa.
I want to use this
Quiero usar esto
I need to know where is the house
Necesito saber dónde es la casa
I need to decide between both places
Necesito decidir entre los dos lugares.
I need to know that everything is ok
Necesito saber que todo está bien

*"That" / "which" can also be used as relative pronouns. The translation in Spanish is *que*. "I need to know that everything is ok" / *Necesito saber que todo está bien.*

Because	Porque
To buy	Comprar
Like this	Así
Them | They	(M) Ellos / (F) Ellas
I can / Can I	Puedo
Book	Libro
Mine	Mío
To understand	Entender / Comprender
Problem / Problems	Problema / problemas
I do / I am doing	Yo hago / Estoy Haciendo
Of	Del
To look	Mirar
Myself	Yo mismo
Enough	Bastante / Suficiente
Food	Comida
Water	Agua
Hotel	Hotel

I like this hotel because I want to look at the beach
Me gusta este hotel porque yo quiero mirar a la playa.
I want to buy a bottle of water
Quiero comprar una botella de agua
I do it like this each day
Yo lo hago así cada día.
Both of them have enough food
Ambos de ellos tienen bastante comida.
That is the book, and that book is mine
Esto es el libro, y este libro es mío.
I need to understand the problem
Yo necesito entender el problema
I have a view of the city from the hotel
Yo tengo una vista de la ciudad del hotel.
I can work today
Yo puedo trabajar hoy.
I do my homework
Yo hago mi tarea.

I like	Me Gusta
There is / There are	Hay
Family / Parents	Familia / Padres
Why	Por qué
To say	Decir
Something	Algo
To go	Ir
Ready	Listo
Soon	Pronto
To work	Trabajar
Who	Quien
To know	Saber

I like to be at my house with my parents
Me gusta estar en la casa con mis padres.
I want to know why I need to say something important
Quiero saber por qué yo necesito decir algo importante.
I am there with him
Estoy allí con él
I am busy, but I need to be ready soon
Estoy ocupado, pero necesito estar listo pronto.
I like to work
Me gusta trabajar
Who is there?
¿Quien está allí?
I want to know if they are here, because I want to go outside
Quiero saber si están aquí, porque yo quiero ir afuera.
There are seven dolls
Hay siete muñecas

How much	Cuánto
To bring	Traer
With me	Conmigo
Instead	En vez
Only	Solamente / sólo
When	Cuando
Lunch	Almuerzo
Or	O
Were	Eran / estaban
Without me	Sin mí
Fast / Quickly	Rápido
Slow / slowly	Despacio
Cold	Frío
Inside	Adentro / dentro
To eat	Comer
Hot	Caliente
To Drive	Manajar

How much money do I need to bring with me?
¿Cuánto dinero necesito llevar conmigo?
Instead of this cake, I like that cake
Envés que esta torta, me gusta esa torta.
Only when you can
Solamente cuando puedes.
They were without me yesterday
Ellos estaban sin mí ayer
I need to drive the car very fast or very slowly
Necesito manejar el auto muy rápido o muy lento.
It is cold inside of the library
Es frío dentro de la biblioteca.
Yes, I like to eat this hot for my lunch
Sí, me gusta comer esto caliente para mi almuerzo.

To answer	Contestar
To fly	Volar
Like (*preposition*)	Como
To travel	Viajar
To learn	Aprender
How	Cómo
To swim	Nadar
To practice	Practicar
To play	Jugar
To leave	Dejar
Many/much/a lot	Mucho
I go to	Yo voy a
First	Primer
Time / Times	Vez / Veces

I need to answer many questions
Necesito contestar muchas preguntas.
I want to fly today
Quiero volar hoy
I need to learn how to swim at the pool
Necesito aprender cómo nadar en la piscina.
I want to learn everything about how to play better tennis
Yo quiero aprender todo sobre cómo jugar tenis mejor.
I want to leave this here for you when I go to travel the world
Yo quiero dejar esto aquí para ti cuando yo voy a viajar el mundo.
Since the first time
Desde la primera vez
The children are yours
Los niños son tuyos

*The feminine singular form of *mucho* is *mucha*, the masculine plural is *muchos*, and the feminine plural is *muchas*.
*With the knowledge you've gained so far, now try to create your own sentences!

Nobody / Anyone	Nadie
Against	Contra
Us	Nosotros
To visit	Visitar
Mom / Mother	Mamá / Madre
To give	Dar
Which	Cuál
To meet	Conocer
Someone	Alguien
Just	Apenas
To walk	Caminar / Andar
Around	Alrededor
Towards	Hacia
Than	Que
Nothing	Nada

Something is better than nothing
Algo es mejor que nada
I am against him
Estoy en contra de él
We go to visit my family each week
Vamos a visitar a mi familia cada semana.
I need to give you something
Necesito darte algo
Do you want to meet someone?
¿Tú quieres conocer alguien?
I am here on Wednesdays as well
Estoy aquí el miércoles también.
You do this everyday?
Haces esto cada día?
You need to walk around, but not towards the house
Necesitas caminar alrededor, pero no hacia la casa

---

*Que could be translated into "what," "that, "than." To read
more about the uses of que, please refer to page 45.
*In Spanish to signify "on" or "before" days, an el must precede
the word. For example, on Wednesdays / el miércoles.

27

I have / I must	Yo tengo
Don't / Doesn't	No
Friend	Amigo
To borrow	Pedir prestado
To look like	Parecer
Grandfather	Abuelo
To want	Querer
To stay	Quedar
To continue	Continuar
Way	Manera / Camino
That's why	Por eso
To show	Mostrar
To prepare	Preperar
I am not going	No me voy

Do you want to look like Arnold?
¿Quieres parecer como Arnold?
I want to borrow this book for my grandfather
Yo quiero pedir prestado este libro para mi abuelo.
I want to drive and to continue on this way to my house
Quiero manejar y continuar en este camino a mi casa.
I have a friend, that's why I want to stay in Madrid
Tengo un amigo, por esto quiero quedar en Madrid.
I am not going to see anyone here
No me voy a ver nadie aquí
I need to show you how to prepare breakfast
Necesito mostrarte cómo preparar diseño.
Why don't you have the book?
¿Por qué tú no tienes el libro?
That is incorrect, I don't need the car today
Eso es equivocado, yo no necesito el auto hoy.

To remember	Recordar
Your	(S)Tu / (P)Tus
Number	Número
Hour	Hora
Dark / darkness	Oscuro / Oscuridad
About	Sobre
Grandmother	Abuela
Five	Cinco
Minute / Minutes	Minuto / Minutos
More	Más
To think	Pensar
To do	Hacer
To come	Venir
To hear	Escuchar
Last	(M)último /(F)última

You need to remember your number
Necesitas recordar tu número.
This is the last hour of darkness
Ésta es la última hora de oscuridad.
**I want to come and to hear my grandmother
speak Spanish today**
Yo quiero venir y escuchar mi abuela hablar
español hoy.
I need to think more about this, and what to do
Necesito pensar más sobre esto, y qué hacer.
From here until there, it's just five minutes
De aquí hasta allá, es solo cinco minutos.

* In the Spanish language, to signify the possessive adjective "your," we use *tu*, plural *tus*. However, the formal case of "your" is *su*, plural *sus*.

29

To leave	Salir
Again	Otra vez /de nuevo
Spain	España
To take	Coger / Tomar
To try	Tratar
To rent	Alquilar
Without her	Sin Ella
We are	Estamos / Somos
To turn off	Apagar
To ask	Pedir
To stop	Parar / Detener
Permission	Permisio

He must go and rent a house at the beach
Él tiene que ir y alquilar una casa en la playa.
I want to take the test without her
Quiero tomar la prueba sin ella.
We are here a long time
Estamos aquí por mucho tiempo
I need to turn off the lights early tonight
Necesito apagar las luces temprano esta noche.
We want to stop here
Queremos detener aquí
We are from Spain
Somos de España
The same building
El mismo edificio
I want to ask permission in order to leave
Quiero pedir permiso para salir.

To open	Abrir
To buy	Comprar
To pay	Pagar
To clean	Limpiar
Without	Sin
Sister	Hermana
To hope	Esperar
To live	Vivir
Nice to meet you	Gusto en cononcer te
Name	Nombre
Last name	Apellido
To return (from place)	Regressar
To return (an object)	Entregar
Enough	Bastante
Door	Puerta
On	Encima de/ sobre
Our	Nuestro

I need to open the door for my sister
Necesito abrir la puerta para mi hermana.
I need to buy something
Necesito comprar algo.
I want to meet your sisters
Quiero conocer tus hermanas
Nice to meet you, what is your name and your last name?
Gusto en conocerte, cuál es tu nombre y tu apellido?
To hope for the better in the future
Para esperar lo mejor en el futuro.
I want to return from the United States and to live without problems in Barcelona
Quiero volver de los Estados Unidos y vivir sin problemas en Barcelona.
Why are you sad right now?
¿Por qué estás triste en este momento?
Our house is on the mountains
Nuestra casa es encima de las montañas

*This *isn't* a phrase book! The purpose of this book is *solely* to provide you with the tools to create *your own* sentences!

To happen	Occurir
To order	Ordenar
To drink	Beber
Excuse me	Permiso / Disculpa
Child	(M)Niño / (F)Niña
Woman	Mujer
To begin / To start	Comenzar
To finish	Terminar
To help	Ayudar
To smoke	Fumar
To love	Amar
To talk / To Speak	Hablar

This needs to happen today
Esto necesito occurir hoy
Excuse me, my child is here as well
Desculpe, my nino esta aqui tambien.
I need to begin soon to be able to finish at three o'clock in the afternoon
Necesito comenzar pronto poder terminar a las tres en el tarde.
I want to learn how to speak Spanish
Quiero apprender cómo hablar Español
I don't want to smoke again
Yo no quiero fumar otra vez.
I want to help
Quiero ayudar
I love you
Te amo
I see you
Te veo
I need you
Te necesito

*To learn more about the typical uses of *te,* please refer to page 46.
*In Spanish the definition of "to start/begin "can either be *comenzar* or *empezar.*

To read	Leer
To write	Escribir
To teach	Enseñar
To close	Cerrar
To turn on	Encender
To prefer / To choose	Preferir
To put	Poner
Less	Menos
Sun	Sol
Month	Mes
I talk / I speak	Yo Hablo
Exact	(M)Exacto/ (F)Exacta

I need this book to learn how to read and write in Spanish because I want to teach in South America
Necesito este libro y aprender cómo leer y escribir en español porque yo quiero enseñar en Sudamérica.
I want to close the door of the house and not to turn on the light
Quiero cerrar la puerta del la casa y no encender las luces
I want to pay less than you for the dinner
Yo quiero pagar menos que tú por la cena.
I prefer to put the gift here
Yo prefiero poner el regalo aquí.
I speak with the boy and the girl in Spanish
Yo hablo con el niño y la niña en español
There is sun outside today
Hay sol afuera hoy.
Is it possible to know the exact date?
¿Es posible saber la fecha exacta?

*In the English language, adjectives precede the noun, but in Spanish, it's usually the opposite. "Big house" is *casa grande,* "new car" is *coche nuevo,* and "exact date" is *fecha exacta.*

To exchange	Intercambiar
To call	Llamar
Brother	Hermano
Dad	Papá
To sit	Sentar
Together	Juntos
To change	Cambiar
Of course	Por supesto
Welcome	Bienvenido
During	Durante
Years	Años
Sky	Cielo
Up	Arriba
Down / Below	Abajo
Sorry	Perdon
To follow	Seguir
Him /Her	Lo / La
Big	Grande
New	Nuevo
Never	Jamás / Nunca

I never want to exchange this money at the bank
Yo nunca quiero cambiar este dinero en el banco.
I want to call my brother and my dad today
Quiero llamar a mi hermano y a mi papa hoy.
Of course I can come to the theater, and I want to sit together with you and with your sister
Por supuesto puedo venir al teatro, y quiero sentar juntos contigo y con tu hermana.
I need to look below in order to see your new house
Necesito mirar abajo para ver tu casa nueva.
I can see the sky from the window
Puedo ver el cielo desde la ventana.
I am sorry, but he wants to follow her to the store
Lo siento, pero él quiere seguirla a la tienda.

*In Spanish an *a* usually precedes nouns relating to people or animals.
*In Spanish *a* + *el* becomes *al*. This only applies to masculine cases, however. For feminine cases, it's *a la*.

To allow	Dejar
To believe	Creer
Morning	Mañana
Except	Excepto
To promise	Prometer
Good night	Buenas noches
To recognize	Conocer
People	Gente
To move	Mover / Mudar
Far	Distante
Different	Differente
Man	Hombre
To enter	Entrar
To receive	Receiber
Throughout	En todo
Good afternoon	Buenas tardes
Through	A travéz
Free	Gratis

I need to allow him to go with us, he is a different man now
Necesito dejarlo ir con nosotros, porque él es un hombre diferente ahora.
I believe everything except this
Yo creo todo excepto esto.
I must promise to say good night to my parents each night
Tengo que prometer decir buenas noches a mis padres cada noche.
They need to recognize the people from Spain very quickly
Tienen que reconocer a las personas de España muy rápido.
I need to move your cat to a different chair
Necesito mover tu gato a una silla diferente.
They want to enter the competition and receive a free book
Quieren entrar en la competición y recibir un libro gratis.
I see the sun throughout the morning from the kitchen
Veo el sol en la mañana de la cocina.
I go into the house but not through the yard
Entro en la casa, pero no a través del jardín

*The verb "to move" has two translations with two definitions in Spanish: *mover*
and *mudar*. *Mover* indicates motion while *mudar* indicates switching locations, for
example to move to another state, or to another house.
*To learn more about the typical uses of *lo* and *la*, please refer to page 47.
*With the knowledge you've gained so far, now try to create your own sentences!

To wish	Desear
Bad	Mal
To Get	Conseguir
To forget	Olvidar
Everybody	Todos
Although	Aunque
To feel	Sentir
Great	Gran
Next (the following)	Proximo
To like	Gustar
In front	Adelante / En frente
Person	Persona
Behind	Atras / detrás
Well	Bien
See you soon / goodbye	Hasta luego / Adiós
Restaurant	Restaurante
Bathroom	Baño

I don't want to wish you anything bad
No quiero desearte nada mal.
I must forget everybody from my past to feel well
Tengo que olvidar todo el mundo de mi pasado para sentir bien.
I am next to the person behind you
Estoy próximo a la persona detrás de ti.
There is a great person in front of me
Hay una gran persona adelante de mí
I say goodbye to my friends
Yo digo adiós a mis amigos.
In which part of the restaurant is the bathroom?
¿En cual parte del restaurante es el baño?
She must get a car before the next year
Ella tiene que conseguir un coche antes del próximo año
I want to like the house, but it is very small
Quiero gustar la casa, pero es muy pequeña.

*"Wish you," *desear*, the verb, and the *te*, the object, connect. To learn more about the typical uses of *te*, please refer to page 46.

To remove	Sacar
Please	Por favor
Beautiful	Lindo /Bello /Hermoso
To lift	Llevar
Include / Including	Incluir /Incluyendo
Belong	Pertencer
To hold	Mantener /Sostener
To check	Revisar
Small	Pequeño
Real	Verdad
Week	Semana
Size	Tamaño
Even though	Aunque
It	(M) Lo / (F) La
So (as in *then*)	Entonces
So (so as in *so much*)	Tan/ tanto
Price	Precio

She wants to remove this door please
Ella quiere sacar esta puerta por favor.
This doesn't belong here, I need to check again
Esto no pertenece aquí, necesito revisar otra vez
This week the weather was very beautiful
Esta semana, el clima estaba muy hermoso.
I need to know which is the real diamond
Necesito saber cuál es el diamante real.
We need to check the size of the house
Necesitamos revisar el tamaño de la casa.
I want to lift this, so you must hold it high
Quiero levantar esto, entonces tienes que sostenerlo alto.
I can pay this although the price is expensive
Puedo pagar esto aunque el precio es caro
Including everything is this price correct
¿Incluyendo todo, este precio es correcto?

Lindo /bello /hermoso is the masculine form of "beautiful, pretty."
The feminine form is *Linda /bella /hermosa.* "Handsome" is *guapo.*

BUILDING BRIDGES

In Building Bridges, we take six conjugated verbs that have been selected after studies I have conducted for several months in order to determine which verbs are most commonly conjugated, and which are then automatically followed by an infinitive verb. For example, once you know how to say, "I need," "I want," "I can," and "I like," you will be able to connect words and say almost anything you want more correctly and understandably. The following three pages contain these six conjugated verbs in first, second, third, fourth, and fifth person, as well as some sample sentences. Please master the entire program up until here prior to venturing onto this section.

I want	Quiero
I need	Necesito
I can	Puedo
I like	Me gusta
I go	Yo voy / Me voy
I have / I must	Tengo / tengo que

I want to go to sleep.
Quiero ir a dormir.
I can go with you to the bus station
Puedo ir contigo a la estación de autobuses.
I need to walk outside of the museum
Necesito caminar fuera del museo.
I like to eat an orange
Me gusta comer una naranja.
I am going to teach a class
Yo voy a enseñar una clase.
I have to speak to my teacher
Tengo que hablar con mi maestro.

Please master pages 16-39, prior to attempting the following two pages!!

You want / do you want	Quieres
He wants / does he want	Quiere
She wants / does she want	Quiere
We want / do we want	Queremos
They want / do they want	Quieren
You (plural) want	Quieren

You need / do you need	Necesitas
He needs / does he need	Necesita
She needs / does she need	Necesita
We want / do we want	Necesitamos
They need / do they need	Necesitan
You (plural) need	Necesitan

You can / can you	Puedes
He can / can he	Puede
She can / can she	Puede
We can / can we	Podemos
They can / can they	Pueden
You (plural) can	Pueden

You like / do you like	Gustas
He likes / does he like	Gusta
She like / does she like	Gusta
We like / do we like	Gustamos
They like / do they like	Gustan
You (plural) like	Gustan

You go / do you go	Vas
He goes / does he go	Va
She goes / does she go	Va
We go / do we go	Vamos
They go / do they go	Van
You (plural) go	Van

You have / do you have	Tienes
He has / does he have	Tiene
She has / does she have	Tiene
We have / do we have	Tenemos
They have / do they have	Tienen
You (plural) have	Tienen

Please master pages 16-39, prior to attempting the following!!

Do you want to go?
¿Quieres ir?
Does he want to fly?
¿Él quiere volar?
We want to swim
Queremos nadar
Do they want to run?
Quieren correr
Do you need to clean?
¿Necesitas limpiar?
She needs to sing a song
Necesita cantar una canción
We need to travel
Necesitamos viajar
They don't need to fight
No necesitan luchar
You (plural) need to see
Necesitan ver
Can you hear me?
¿Puedes escucharme?
He can dance very well
Puede bailar muy bien
We can go out tonight
Podemos salir esta noche
They can break the wood
Pueden romper la madera
Do you like to eat here?
¿Gustas comer aquí?

He likes to spend time here
Él gusta pasar tiempo aquí
We like to fix the house
Gustamos arreglar la casa
They like to cook
Gustan cocinar
You (plural) like my house
Gustan mi casa
Do you go to school today?
¿Vas a la escuela hoy?
He goes fishing
Él va a pescar
We are going to relax
Vamos a relajar
They go to watch a film
Van a ver una película
Do you have money?
¿Tienes dinero?
She has to look outside
Ella tiene que mirar afuera
We have to sign our names
Tenemos que firmar
nuestros nombres
They have to send the letter
Tienen que enviar la carta
You (plural) have to order
Tienen que ordenar

BASIC GRAMMATICAL REQUIREMENTS OF THE SPANISH LANGUAGE WHICH YOU WILL ENCOUNTER IN THIS PROGRAM

In Spanish, nouns are plural or singular as well as masculine or feminine. For example, the article "the" for Spanish nouns ending with an a, e, and i (usually deemed as feminine) is typically *la*. For nouns ending with an o, the noun is generally masculine, and the article is usually *el*.

The article "the" in plural form is *los* for masculine forms and *las* for feminine forms. "The boy" is *el* (the) *niño* (boy), "the girl" is *la niña*, "the boys" is *los niños*, and "the girls" is *las niñas*. Although most Spanish words that end with an a are usually feminine and those that end with an o are generally masculine ("the house" is *la casa*, "the car" is *el auto*), there are exceptions. For words that end with ma, pa, and ta, the article is usually *el*. For example, "the problem" is *el problema* and not *la problema*.

For the article "a" *(un and una)*, its conjugation is determined by feminine and masculine forms, "a car"— *un auto*, "a house"—*una casa*. The conjugation for "this" *(esta, este, estos, and estas)* and "that" *(ese, esa, esos, esas)* is similar. "This," *este*, is masculine, for example, *este libro* ("this book"). Feminine is *esta*, for instance, *esta casa* ("this house"). *Estos libros* ("these books") and *estas casas* ("these houses") is the plural form. "That," *ese*, is masculine, that is, *ese libro* (that book). Feminine would be *esa*, for example, *esa silla* ("that chair"). In plural, this is *esos libros* ("those books) and *esas sillas* ("those chairs").

Eso and *esto* are neuter pronouns, meaning they don't have a gender. They usually refer to an idea or an unknown object that isn't specifically named, for example, "that"/ *eso;* "that is"/ *eso es;* "because of that" / *por eso;* "this" / *esto;* "this is good" / *esto es bien;* and "what is this?" / *qué es esto?*

In regards to "my," singular and plural form exists as well, *mi* and *mis.*

    "my chair" / *mi silla*

    "my chairs" / *mis sillas*

With regard to "your," tu and tus, the singular is tu, as in tu auto / "your car," and the plural is tus (e.g., tus autos / your cars).

Temporary and Permanent

The different forms of "is" are *es* and *esta.* When referring to a permanent condition, for example, "she is a girl" (*ella* es *una niña),* you use *es.* For temporary positions, "the girl is doing well today" *(la chica esta muy bien hoy),* you use *esta.* "You are" or "are you" could be translated as *estas,* or they could also be translated as *tú eres.* An example of temporary position is "how are you today?" *(cómo estas hoy).* And another example of temporary position is "you are here" *(estas aquí).* Another example of permanent position is "are you Mexican?" *(tú eres Mexicano?)* as well as "you are a man!" *(tú eres un hombre!).* Both derive from the verbs *ser* (permanent) and *estar* (temporary).

    "I am"—estoy and yo soy. *Yo soy* refers to a permanent condition: "I am Italian" / *Yo soy Italiano.* Temporary condition would be "I am at the mall" / *Estoy en el mall.*

    "We are"—somos (permanent) and estamos (temporary). *Somos Peruvianos* / "we are Peruvian" *and estamos en el parque* / "we are at the park."

    "They are"—son (permanent) and estan (temporary). *Ellos son Chilenos* / "they are Chileans" *and ellos estan en el auto* / "they are in the car."

Synonyms and Antonyms
There are three ways of describing time.
Vez/veces—"first time" / *primera vez* or "three times" / *tres veces*
Tiempo—"during the time of the dinosaurs" / d*urante el tiempo de los dinosaurios*
Hora— "What time is it?" / *Qué hora es?*

Que has four definitions.
"What"—*Que es esto?* / "What is this?"
"Than"—*Estoy mejor que tu* / "I am better than you"
"That"—"I want to say that I am near the house" / *yo quiero decir que estoy acerca de la casa*
"I must" / "I have to"—*Tengo que.* The verb *tener*, "to have," whether it's in conjugated or infinite form, if it is followed by an infinitive verb, then *que* must always follow.
For example:

"I have to swim now" / *tengo que nadar ahora.*

Dejar has two definitions.
To leave—*Yo quiero dejar esto aquí* / "I want to leave this here" (*Dejar* is to leave something, but when saying "to leave" as in "going," it's "*salir*," for example, "I want to leave now" / *quiero salir ahora.*)
To allow—*Dejar* could also mean to allow.

There are two ways of describing "so."
"So"—*entonces.* "So I need to know" / *entonces necesito saber.*
"So"—*tan. Eso es tan distante* / "this is so far"

Si and Sí
Si (without accent) means "if"
Sí (with accent) means "yes"

Verb Conjugation

The word "I" (yo) before a conjugated verb isn't required. For example, *yo necesito saber la fecha* ("I need to know the date") can be said, *Necesito saber la fecha* because *necesito* already means "I need" in conjugated form, although saying yo isn't incorrect! The same can also be said with *tú / te, el / ella, nosotros, ellos / ellas,* in which they aren't required to be placed prior to the conjugated verb, but if they are, then it isn't considered wrong.

Ir a + infinitive and *yo voy* & *me voy*

In Spanish "to," a (pronounced as "ha"), isn't required between the conjugated verb and the infinitive form. For example, *puedo decir* ("I can say"). But in regards to the verb "to go", *ir*, the preposition a must always follow the *ir* (whether in the conjugated or infinitive form) before connecting with the infinitive verb. For example, *voy a ver* ("I am going to see") or *Yo necesito ir a buscar* ("I need to go to search"). "I go" and "I am going" could either be translated as *yo voy* or *me voy*. *Yo voy* refers to going to a specific place, for example, *yo voy a la tienda* ("I am going to the store"). *Me voy* is going somewhere and not specifying the exact destination, for example, *me voy afuera* ("I am going outside").

Tú, Te, Ti and *Tu*

There are three different forms of how to use the pronoun "you"—*tú, te,* and *ti*.

Tú is a subject pronoun (second person of singular), referring to the individual who is doing the action. Unlike in English, it isn't required in Spanish. For example, in "you are here" / *estas aquí*, you aren't required to say *tú estas aquí*.

Te is a direct and indirect object pronoun, the person who is actually affected by the action that is being carried out. But the te comes before the verb, for example, "I send you" / *te mando* or "I permit you" / *te permito*. In the event the verb is infinitive, then *te* precedes the verb. For example, in the sentence "I want to follow you" / *quiero seguirte, seguir* and the *te* will connect with the verb and become one word.

Ti is a preposition pronoun, meaning it goes with a preposition (like *para, de, por),* for example, *para ti* / "for you" or *yo voy a ti* / "I am going to you" (added a *ti*).

Tu without the accent (´) means "your": *tu casa* / "your house."

Tuyo means "yours" and *tuyos* is plural, for example, *el libro es tuyo* / "the book is yours" and "the books are yours" / *los libros son tuyos.*

The following page is an advanced section of this program, please don't proceed unless you mastered everything up until here!

Using De

De is one of the most crucial prepositions in the Spanish language. Its most common use is much like the English words "from" and "of," but you will encounter it in other situations as well. It could also mean "than," "in," "with," and "by."

Use *de* when referring to "of" and "from."

·   "I am from the United States" / *Soy de los Estados Unidos.*
·   "three more days of summer" / *tres más días de verano*

Using *de* as than

     Estoy mejor de tu. / "I am better than you."

Another form of *de* is to indicate the possessor.

    la casa de Moises / "Moises's house" or "the house of Moises"
    las playas de Florida / "Florida's beaches" or "the beaches of Florida"

Another use for *de* is for preposition phrases.

    afuera de la casa de tu novia / "outside the house of your girlfriend"
a lado de tu novio / "next to your boyfriend"
alrededor de la picina / "around the pool"

This should cover the most typical uses of *de*. However, there are other uses which haven't been mentioned here.

Using Lo and La

Lo and *La* are used as direct masculine, feminine, and neuter object pronouns, meaning "him," "her," or "it."

In case the verb is conjugated, *lo* and *la* precede the conjugated verb.

    "I don't want him to know" / *no lo quiero conocer*

    "I don't need her" / *No la necesito"

    "I want it" / *lo quiero*

    "I bought it" / *lo compré*

If the verb is in the infinitive form, then the *lo* and the *la* precede the infinitive verb and connect, creating one word:

    "I want to buy it." / *Quiero comprarlo.*
    "I want to find it." / *Quiero encontrarlo.*
    "I want to see her." / *Quiero verla.*
    "I don't want to know him." / *No quiero conocerlo.*
    "I don't want to give her." / *No quiero darla.*

Another example of using *lo* in Spanish, is, as the abstract neuter article "the".

    "the best of Charlie Chaplin" / *lo mejor de Charlie Chaplin*
(since "best" is the abstract neuter noun)

OTHER USEFUL TOOLS FOR
THE SPANISH LANGUAGE

Reading and Pronunciation

The pronunciation of Spanish, in comparison to the English language, is more or less the same. There are, however, a few exceptions that are listed below. Please read and familiarize yourself with the rules of Spanish pronunciation.

CE is pronounced as *se*. *Él dice* is pronounced as "él di-se."

G when followed by *e* or *i* sounds like the letter *h* in English, like hot. For example *general* is pronounced as he-nere-ral.

H is silent - For example, *hacer* is pronounced as acer

J is pronounced similar to the *ch* in German and in Hebrew ("loch," "channuka," and "yacht"). For example, the English word "garden", translated jardin in Spanish, would sound like "chardin." The sound is a little difficult to pronounce for non-Spanish speakers. Tip: pronounce as if you are coughing up phlegm in the back of your throat. The English word "job", translated *trabajo*, is pronounced as "tra-ba-cho."

Ñ is pronounced as "ny." For example, "morning," *mañana*, sounds like "ma-ny-ana."

LL is pronounced as je for example to arrive, *llegar*, it sounds like je-gar. Although in some Spanish countries they pronounce it as ye; *llegar* would be pronounced as ye-gar.

RR is hard to pronounce for non-Spanish speakers, but an easy Tip is that the pronunciation is similar to the sound of a starting car engine, "rrrrrr." "Dog," *perro*, would be pronounced as "pe-rrrr-o."

V is pronounced as "b." *Victor* would be pronounced as "Biktor."

Z is pronounced as "s." For example shoe, *zeta*, would be pronounced as "seta."

Days of the Week

Sunday	Domingo
Monday	Lunes
Tuesday	Martes
Wednesday	Miércoles
Thursday	Jueves
Friday	Viernes
Saturday	Sábado

Seasons

Spring	Primavera
Summer	Verano
Autumn	Otoño
Winter	Invierno

Cardinal Directions

North	Norte
South	Sur
East	Este
West	Oeste

Colors

Black	Negro
White	Blanco
Gray	Gris
Red	Rojo
Blue	Azul
Yellow	Amarillo
Green	Verde
Orange	Naranja
Purple	Purpura
Brown	Marrón

Numbers

One	Uno
Two	Dos
Three	Tres
Four	Cuatro
Five	Cinco
Six	Sies
Seven	Siete
Eight	Ocho
Nine	Nueve
Ten	Diez

Conversational
French
Quick and Easy

**THE MOST INNOVATIVE AND REVOLUTIONARY
TECHNIQUE TO MASTER CONVERSATIONAL FRENCH**

YATIR NITZANY

THE FRENCH LANGUAGE

The French language originated in France. It is a Romance language as are Spanish, Portuguese, Italian, and Romanian since they all descend from what originally was the spoken Latin language. In the sixteenth century, King Francis I declared French as his nation's official language. Little did he know it was soon to become the fifteenth most-common language in the world and the official language of almost thirty countries.

The French language was once used in diplomatic circles and was also a symbol of prestige, meaning only the nobility and higher classes of educated people spoke it. Russia's Catherine the Great and all her court communicated in French, as well as Prussia's Frederick II. Today, because of France's colonial expansion between the seventeenth and twentieth centuries, there are now twenty-nine countries where French is the official language. Despite its many dialects French is still spoken in all its former colonies. However, the language has declined in popularity since its peak in the sixteen and seventeenth centuries. But French is again rising in popularity. It has sixteen million students and 220 million native speakers.

Spoken in: France, Belgium, Switzerland, Luxembourg, Monaco, Benin, Burkina Faso, Burundi, Cameroon, Canada, Central African Republic, Chad, Comoros, Republic of the Congo, Democratic Republic of the Congo, Côte d'Ivoire, Djibouti, Equatorial Guinea, Gabon, Guiana, Guinea, Haiti, Madagascar, Mali, Niger, Rwanda, Senegal, Seychelles, Togo, and Vanuatu

MEMORIZATION MADE EASY

There is no doubt the three hundred and fifty words in my program are the required essentials in order to engage in quick and easy basic conversation in any foreign language. However, some people may experience difficulty in the memorization. For this reason, I created Memorization Made Easy. This memorization technique will make this program so simple and fun that it's unbelievable! I have spread the words over the following twenty pages. Each page contains a vocabulary table of ten to fifteen words. Below every vocabulary box, sentences are composed from the words on the page that you have just studied. This aids greatly in memorization. Once you succeed in memorizing the first page, then proceed to the second page. Upon completion of the second page, go back to the first and review. Then proceed to the third page. After memorizing the third, go back to the first and second and repeat. And so on. As you continue, begin to combine words and create your own sentences in your head. Every time you proceed to the following page, you will notice words from the previous pages will be present in those simple sentences as well, because repetition is one of the most crucial aspects in learning any foreign language. Upon completion of your twenty pages, congratulations, you have absorbed the required words and gained a basic, quick-and-easy proficiency and you should now be able to create your own sentences and say anything you wish in French. This is a crash course in conversational French, and it works!

For further assistance in the memorization and pronunciation of the vocabulary of this program, you may also purchase the audio version of this book which is featured on Audible, iTunes, and Amazon.

NOTE TO THE READER

The purpose of this book is merely to enable you to communicate in French. In the program itself (pages 16-40) you may notice that the composition of some of those sentences might sound rather clumsy. This is intentional. These sentences were formulated in a specific way to serve two purposes: to facilitate the easy memorization of the vocabulary and to teach you how to combine the words in order to form your own sentences for quick and easy communication, rather than making complete literal sense in the English language. So keep in mind that this is not a phrase book!

As the title suggests, the sole purpose of this program is for conversational use only. It is based on the mirror translation technique. These sentences, as well as the translations are not incorrect, just a little clumsy. Latin languages, Semitic languages, and Anglo-Germanic languages, as well as a few others, are compatible with the mirror translation technique.

Many users say that this method surpasses any other known language learning technique that is currently out there on the market. Just stick with the program and you will achieve wonders!

Again, I wish to stress this program is by no means, shape, or form a phrase book! The sole purpose of this book is to give you a fundamental platform to enable you to connect certain words to become conversational. Please also read the "Introduction" and the "About Me" section prior to commencing the program.

In order to succeed with my method, please start on the very first page of the program and fully master one page at a time prior to proceeding to the next. Otherwise, you will overwhelm yourself and fail. Please do not skip pages, nor start from the middle of the book.

It is a myth that certain people are born with the talent to learn a language, and this book disproves that myth. With this method, anyone can learn a foreign language as long as he or she follows these explicit directions:

* Memorize the vocabulary on each page

* Follow that memorization by using a notecard to cover the words you have just memorized and test yourself.

* Then read the sentences following that are created from the vocabulary bank that you just mastered.

* Once fully memorized, give yourself the green light to proceed to the next page.

Again, if you proceed to the following page without mastering the previous, you are guaranteed to gain nothing from this book. If you follow the prescribed steps, you will realize just how effective and simplistic this method is.

THE PROGRAM

Let's Begin! "Vocabulary"
(Memorize the Vocabulary)

I | I am	Je | Je suis
With you	Avec vous / Avec toi
With him / with her	Avec il / Avec elle
With us	Avec nous
For you	Pour vous / Pour toi
Without him	Sans lui
Without them	(Masc.) Sans eux / (fem)Sans Elles
Always	Toujours
Was	Etait
This	Ça, Ce, (Masc)Celui (Fem) Cela
Is	Est
Sometimes	Quelques fois / parfois
Maybe	Peut être
Are you	Êtes-vous / Es-tu
Better	Mieux / Meilleur
His / Hers	Que lui /qu'elle
He / She	Il / Elle
From	De

Sentences composed from the vocabulary (now you can speak the sentences and combine the words).

I am with you

Je suis avec toi

This is for you

C'est pour toi

I am from Canada

Je suis de Canada

Are you from Canada?

Êtes-vous de Canada?

Sometimes you are with us at the mall

Parfois tu es avec nous au mall

I am always with her

Je suis toujours avec elle

Are you without them today?

Êtes-vous sans eux aujourd'hui?

Sometimes I am with him

Quelques fois je suis avec lui

*Concerning the demonstrative "that" / ça, ce, cela, please read page 86.
*Mall is a universal known term in all languages, but the correct form of saying "mall" in French is centre commercial.

I was	J'étais
To be	Être
The	Le/ La/ Les / au
Same	Même
Good	Bon
Here	Ici
It's / it is	C'est / il est
And	Et
Between	Entre
Now	Maintenant
Later / After	Plus tard
If	Si
Yes	Oui
Then	Alors
Tomorrow	Demain
You	**(formal)** Vous/ **(informal)** tu
Also / too / as well	Aussi

Between now and later
Entre maintenant et plus tard
If it's later, then it is better tomorrow
Si c'est plus tard, alors il vaut mieux demain
This is good as well
C'est bon aussi
To be the same
Être le même
Yes, you are very good
Oui, vous êtes très bon
I was here with them
J'étais ici avec eux.
You and I
Vous et moi
The same day
Le même jour

*Concerning the formal and informal forms of *you*; *tu* and *vous*, please refer to page 84.
*The masculine form of the article "the" is *le*, the feminine form is *la*, and plural form is *les*.
*The definition of *"au"* is "to the." Please read page 83 to learn more.

Me	Moi
Ok	Ok
Even if	Même si
Afterwards	Ensuite
Worse	Pire
Where	Où
Everything	Tout / tous
Somewhere	Quelque part
What	Quoi?
Almost	Presque
There	Là / là-bas

Afterwards is worse
Ensuite est pire
Even if I go now
Même si j'y vais maintenant?
Where is everything?
Où est tout?
Maybe somewhere
Peut être quelque part
What? I am almost there
Quoi? Je suis presque là
Where are you?
Vous êtes où?

House	Maison
In	Dans / en
Car	Voiture
Already	Déja
Good morning	Bonjour
How are you?	Comment ça va?
Where are you from?	D'où vous venez?
Today	Aujourd'ui
Hello	Bonjour
What is your name?	Comment tu t'appelles?
How old are you?	Quel est votre âge?
Son	Fils
Daughter	Fille
At	À
Very	Très
Hard	Dur
Still	Encore

She is without a car, so maybe she is still at the house?
Elle n'a pas de voiture, alors peut-être qu'elle est encore
à la maison
I am in the car already with your son and daughter
Je suis déjà dans la voiture avec ton fils et fille
Good morning, how are you today?
Bonjour, comment ça va aujourd'ui?
Hello, what is your name?
Bonjour, comment tu t'appelles?
How old are you?
Quel est votre age?
This is very hard, but it's not impossible
C'est très dur, mais ce n'est pas impossible
Where are you from?
D'où venez vous?

*In French the word "so" has two definitions; *alors* and *si*.
Alors means "then" while *si* indicates "so much" or "very."

Thank you	Merci
For	Pour
Anything	Quelque chose
This is	C'est
Time	Temps
But	Mais
No / Not	Non
I am not	Je ne suis pas
Away	Loin
That	Ça (M) Ce, (F) Cela
Similar	Similaire
Other / Another	Autre / une autre
Side	Côté
Until	Jusque / jusqu'à
Yesterday	Hier
Without us	Sans nous
Since	Depuis
Day	Jour
Before	Avant

Thanks for anything
Merci pour quelque chose
It's almost time
C'est presque temps
I am not here, I am away
Je ne suis pas ici, je suis loin
That is a similar house
C'est une maison similaire
I am from the other side
Je suis de l'autre côté
But I was here until late yesterday
Mais j'étais ici jusque tard hier
Since the other day
Depuis l'autre jour

*Concerning the demonstrative "that" / *ça, ce, cela,* please read page 86.

I say / I am saying	Je dis que / Je suis en train de dire
What time is it?	Quelle heure est-il?
I want	Je veux
Without you	Sans toi
Everywhere /wherever	Partout / Partout où
I go / I am going	Je vais/ Je suis en train d'aller
With	Avec
My	(Sing M/F) Mon/Ma (Plu) Mes
Cousin	Cousin
I need	J'ai besoin
Right now	Maintenant
Night	Nuit
To see	Voir
Light	Lumière
Outside	Dehors
That is	C'est
Any	(Sing) Quelque (Plu) Quelques
I see / I am seeing	Je vois

I am saying no / I say no
Je suis en train de dire non / Je dis non
I want to see this during the day
Je veux voir cela pendant la journée
I see this everywhere
Je vois ça partout
I am happy without any of my cousins here
Je suis très content sans aucun de mes cousins ici
I need to be there at night
J'ai besoin d'être là la nuit
I see light outside
Je vois de la lumière dehors
What time is it right now?
Quelle heure est-il maintenant?

*This *isn't* a phrase book! The purpose of this book is *solely* to provide you with the tools to create *your own* sentences!
*Any (Sing) - *Quelque* (Plu) *Quelques* (both plural and singular form pronounced as quelque since the final "s" in *quelques* is silent), please see page 87 to learn more.

Place	Lieu
Easy	Facile
To find	Trouver
To look for/to search	Chercher
Near / Close	Près de
To wait	Attendre
To sell	Vendre
To use	Utiliser
To know	Savoir
To decide	Décider
Between	Entre
Two	Deux
To	À /à

This place is easy to find
Ce lieu est facile à trouver
I need to look for you next to the car
J'ai besoin de vous chercher près de la voiture
I am saying to wait until tomorrow
Je dis d'attendre jusqu'à demain
It's easy to sell this table
C'est facile de vendre cette table
I want to use this
Je veux utiliser ça
I need to know where is the house
J'ai besoin de savoir où est la maison
I need to decide between both places
J'ai besoin de décider entre les deux endroits
I need to know that everything is ok
J'ai besoin de savoir que tout est ok

"That" and "which" can also be used as relative pronouns. The translation in French is *que*. "I need to know **that** everything is ok" / *j'ai besoin de savoir que tout est ok.*

Because	Parce que
To buy	Acheter
Both	Les deux
Them | They	(M) Eux (F) Elles / (M) Ils (F) elles
Their	Leurs
Book	Livre
Mine	À moi / le mien
To understand	Comprendre
Problem / Problems	Problème
I do / I am doing	Je fais/ Je suis en train de faire
Of	De
To look	Regarder
Myself	Moi même
Enough	Assez
Food	Nourriture
Water	Eau
Hotel	Hotel

I like this hotel because I want to look at the beach
J'aime cet hôtel parce que je veux regarder la plage
I want to buy a bottle of water
Je veux acheter une bouteille d'eau
I do it like this each day
Je fais comme ça tous les jours
Both of them have enough food
Tous les deux ont suffisament de nourriture
That is the book, and that book is mine
C'est le livre, et ce livre est le mien
I need to understand the problem
J'ai besoin de comprendre le problème
From the hotel I have a view of the city
Depuis l'hôtel j'ai une vue de la ville
I can work today
Je peux travailler aujourd'hui
I do my homework
Je fais mes devoirs

For the conjugation of "they have" / *ont*, please refer to the page 81 & 82.

I like	J'aime
There is / There are	Il y a
Family / Parents	Famille/ Parents
Why	Porquoi
To say	Dire
Something	Quelque chose
To go	Aller
Ready	Prêt
Soon	Bientôt
To work	Travailler
Who	Qui
To know	Savoir

I like to be at my house with my parents
J'aime être à la maison avec mes parents
I want to know why I need to say something important
Je veux savoir pourquoi j'ai besoin de dire quelque chose
d'important
I am there with him
Je suis là-bas avec lui
I am busy, but I need to be ready soon
Je suis occupé, mais j'ai besoin d'être prêt bientôt
I like to go to work
J'aime aller travailler
Who is there?
Qui là-bas?
I want to know if they are here, because I want to go outside
Je veux savoir s'ils sont ici, parce je veux sortir
There are seven dolls
Il y a sept poupées

*The literal meaning of *sortir* is "to go out."

How much	Combien
To bring	Apporter
With me	Avec moi
Instead	À la place de
Only	Seulement
When	Quand
I can / Can I	Je peux / puis-je?
Or	Ou
Were	Étaient
Without me	Sans moi
Fast	Vite
Slow	Lentement
Cold	Froid
Inside	Dedans / l'intérieur
To eat	Manger
Hot	Chaud
To Drive	Conduire

How much money do I need to bring with me?
Combien d'argent ai-je besoin d'apporter avec moi?
Instead of this cake, I like that cake
À la place de ce gâteau, j'aime l'autre gâteau
Only when you can
Seulement quand tu peux
They were without me yesterday
Ils étaient sans moi hier
I need to drive the car very fast or very slowly
J'ai besoin de conduire la voiture très vite ou très lentement
It is cold inside the library
Il fait froid à l'intérieur de la bibliothèque
Yes, I like to eat this hot for my lunch
Oui, j'aime manger ça chaud pour mon déjeuner

*"Instead / *à la place de* literally translates to "in place of."

To answer	Répondre
To fly	Voler
Today	Aujourd'ui
To travel	Voyager
To learn	Aprendre
How	Comment
To swim	Nager
To practice	Practiquer
To play	Jouer
To leave	Laisser
Many/much/a lot	Beaucoup
I go to	Je vais à
First	Premier
Time / Times	Fois

I need to answer many questions
J'ai besoin de répondre à beaucoup de questions
The bird must fly
L'oiseau doit voler
I need to learn to swim at the pool
J'ai besoin d'apprendre à nager à la piscine
I want to learn everything about how to play better tennis
Je veux tout savoir sur comment mieux jouer au tennis
I want to leave this here for you when I go to travel the world
Je veux laisser ça ici pour toi quand je vais voyager autour du monde
Since the first time
Depuis la première fois
The children are yours
Les enfants sont les votres

*In French, the verb "to leave" has two meanings: *laisser* and *partir*.
* "to leave (something)" / *laisser*
* "to leave (a place/to go)" / *partir*
*With the knowledge you've gained so far, now try to create your own sentences!

Nobody / Anyone	Personne
Against	Contre
Us	Nous
To visit	Rendre visite à
Mom / Mother	Maman/ Mère
To give	Donner
Which	Lequel
To meet	Rencontrer
Someone	Quelqu'un
Just	À peine
To walk	Marcher
Around	Autour
Towards	Vers
Than	Que
Nothing / Anything	Rien

Something is better than nothing
Quelque chose est mieux que rien
I am against him
Je suis contre lui
We go to visit my family each week
Nous allons rendre visite à ma famille chaque semaine
I need to give you something
J'ai besoin de te donner quelque chose
Do you want to meet someone?
Voulez-vous rencontrer quelqu'un?
I am here on Wednesdays as well
Je suis ici les mercredis aussi
You do this everyday?
Vous faites cela tous les jours?
You have to walk around, but not towards the house
Vous avez de marcher autour mais non vers la maison

*In French, "you want" is vous voulez, but "do you want" is voulez-vouz. Please refer 81 and 82 to learn more.

*In French, the word "which," the masculine form is *lequel*. *Laquelle* is the feminine form. *Lesquels* is the masculine plural, and *lesquelles* is the feminine plural.

I have	J'ai
Don't	Ne (...) pas
Friend	(M)Ami/ (F)Amie
To borrow	Emprunter
To look like	Avoir l'air de / ressembler à
Grandfather	Grand père
To want	Vouloir
To stay	Rester
To continue	Continuer
Way	Chemin(*road*)/manière(*method*)
That's why	C'est pourquoi
To show	Montrer
To prepare	Préparer
I am not going	Je ne vais pas

Do you want to look like Arnold

Voulez-vous ressembler à Arnold?

I want to borrow this book for my grandfather

Je veux emprunter ce livre pour mon grand père

I want to drive and to continue on this way to my house

Je veux conduire et continuer sur ce chemin jusqu'à chez moi

I have a friend, that's why I want to stay in Paris

J'ai un amie, c'est pour cela que je veux rester à Paris

I am not going to see anyone here

Je ne vais pas voir personne ici

I need to show you how to prepare breakfast

J'ai besoin de te montrer comment préparer le petit déjeuner

Why don't you have the book?

Pourquoi n'avez vous pas le livre?

That is incorrect, I don't need the car today

C'est incorrect, je n'ai pas besoin de la voiture aujourd'hui

*In French friend is *ami,* plural form for male is *amis* and plural form for female is *amies.*
*To make a verb negative, add *ne* before the verb and pas after. Please see page 86 to learn more.
Chez moi means "home" while *maison* means "house."
*In French there are two forms of expressing "way": *chemin,* meaning "road"; or, *maniere,* meaning "method."

To remember	Se rappeler de
Your	(Sing)(M)Ton /(F)Ta (Plur)Tes
Number	Numéro
Hour	L'heure
Dark / darkness	Sombre / Oscurité
About	A / À propos / sur
Grandmother	Grand mère
Five	Cinq
Minute / Minutes	Minute / Minutes
More	Plus
To think	Penser
To do	Faire
To come	Venir
To hear	Écouter
Last	(M)Dernièr /(F)Dernière

You need to remember my number
Vous avez besoin de vous rappeler de mon numéro
This is the last hour of darkness
C'est la dernière heure d'obscurité
I want to come and to hear my grandmother speak French today
Je veux venir et écouter ma grand-mère parle français aujourd'hui
I need to think more about this, and what to do
J'ai besoin de penser plus à ça, et quoi faire
From here until there, it's only five minutes
D'ici jusque la, c'est seulement çinq minutes
I must go to sleep
Je dois aller dormir
Where is the airport?
Ou est l'aéroport?

To leave	Partir
Again	Encore
France	France
To take	Prendre
To try	Essayer
To rent	Louer
Without her	Sans elle
We are	Nous sommes
To turn off	Eteindre
To ask	Demander
To stop	Arrêter
Permission	Permission

He needs to leave and rent a house at the beach
Il a besoin de partir et louer une maison à la plage
I want to pass the test without her
Je veux passer le test sans elle
We are here a long time
Nous sommes ici depuis longtemps
I need to turn off the lights early tonight
J'ai besoin d'éteindre les lumières tôt ce soir
We want to stop here
Nous voulons nous arrêter ici
We came from Spain
Nous venons d'Espagne
The same building
Le même immeuble
I want to ask permission to leave
Je veux demander la permission de partir

*In French, "night" is *nuit*, but "tonight" is *ce soir*.

To open	Ouvrir
To buy	Acheter
To pay	Payer
Last	Dernier
Without	Sans
Sister	Sœur
To hope	Espérer
To live	Vivre
Nice to meet you	Ravis de faire votre connaisance
Name	Prénom
Last name	Nom
To return	Retourner
Enough	Assez
Door	Porte

I need to open the door for my sister
J'ai besoin d'ouvrir la porte pour ma sœur
I need to buy something
J'ai besoin d'acheter quelque chose
I want to meet your sisters
Je veux rencontrer tes sœurs
Nice to meet you, what is your name and your last name?
Ravis de faire votre connaissance, quel est votre prénom et votre nom?
To hope for the better in the future
Espèrer le mieux pour l'avenir
I want to return from the United States and to live without problems in France
Je veux retourner aux États-Unis et vivre sans problèmes en France
Why are you sad right now?
Pourquoi êtes-vous triste maintenant?
Our house is on the hill
Notre maison est sur la colline

*The plural form of "your" is *tes*. The masculine singular of "your" is *ton*. The feminine form is *ta*. The formal is *votre*. Read page 84 to learn more.
*This *isn't* a phrase book! The purpose of this book is *solely* to provide you with the tools to create *your own* sentences!

To happen	Arriver
To order	Commander
To drink	Boire
Excuse me	Excusez-moi
Child	Enfant
Woman	Femme
To begin / To start	Commencer
To finish	Finir
To help	Aider
To smoke	Fumer
To love	Aimer
To talk / To Speak	Parler

This must happen today
Cela doit arriver aujourd'hui
Excuse me, my child is here as well
Excusez-moi, mon enfant est ici aussi
I love you
Je vous aime
I see you
Je vous vois
I need you
J'ai besoin de vous
I need to begin soon to be able to finish at 3 o'clock in the afternoon
J'ai besoin de commencer bientôt pour pouvoir finir à 3 heures de l'après-midi
I want to help
Je veux aider
I don't want to smoke again
Je ne veux pas fumer encore
I want to learn to speak French
Je veux apprendre à parler Français

*The verb "must" and the verb "to have to" is *devoir*.
Conjugation form:
* "I want" / *je dois*
* "You want" (informal) / *tu dois*
* "He, she, it wants / *il, elle, cela doit*
* "We want" / *nous devons*
* "You want" (formal) / *vous devez*
* "They want" (regardless masculine or fem) / *ils, elles doivent*

To read	Lire
To choose	Choisir
To write	Écrire
To teach	Enseigner
To close	Fermer
To turn on	Allumer
To prefer	Préférer
To put	Mettre
Less	Moins
Sun	Soleil
Month	Mois
I Talk	Je parle
Exact	Exacte

I need this book to learn how to read and write in French because I want to teach in France
J'ai besoin de ce livre pour apprendre á lire et écrire en Français parce que je veux enseigner en France
I want to close the door of the house and not to turn on the light
Je veux fermer la porte de la maison et ne pas allumer la lumière
I prefer to put the gift here
Je préfère mettre le cadeau ici
I want to pay less than you for the dinner
Je veux payer moins que vous pour le dîner
I speak with the boy and the girl in Spanish
Je parle avec le garçon et la fille en espagnol
There is sun outside today
Il y a du soleil dehors aujourd'hui
Is it possible to know the exact date?
Est-il possible de savoir la date exacte?

*In English, adjectives precede the noun, for example "exact date," but in French it's usually the opposite, *la date exacte.*

To exchange	Échanger
To call	Appeler
Brother	Frère
Dad	Papa
To sit	Asseoir
Together	Ensemble
To change	Changer
Of course	Bien sûr
Welcome	Bienvenue
During	Pendant
Years	Ans
Sky	Ciel
Up	Là-haut
Down	En bas
Sorry	(M)Désolé/(F)Désolée
To follow	Suivre
Him / Her	(M)Le/Lui | (F)La/Elle
Big	Grand
New	Nouveau
Never	Jamais

I never want to exchange this money at the bank
Je ne veux jamais échanger cet argent à la banque
I want to call my brother and my dad today
Je veux appeler mon frère et mon papa aujourd'hui
Of course I can come to the theater, and I want to sit together with you and with your sister
Bien sûr je peux venir au théâtre, et je veux m'asseoir ensemble avec vous et ta sœur
I need to go down to see your new house
J'ai besoin d'aller en bas pour voir ta nouvelle maison
I can see the sky from the window
Je peux voir le ciel depuis la fenêtre
I am sorry, but he wants to follow her to the store
Je suis désolé, il veut la suivre au magasin

To allow	Permettre
To believe	Croire
Morning	Matin
Except	Sauf
To promise	Promettre
Good night	Bonsoir/ Bonne soiree
To recognize	Reconnaître
People	Gens
To move	Déplacer / Déménager
Far	Loin
Different	Différent
Man	Homme
To enter	Entrer
To receive	Recevoir
Throughout	Tout au long de
Good afternoon	Bon apres midi
Through	À travers
Him / Her	(M)Le /Lui | (F)La /Elle

I need to allow him to go with us, he is a different man now
J'ai besoin de le laisser partir avec nous, il est un homme différent maintenant

I believe everything except for this
Je crois tout sauf cela

I must promise to say good night to my parents each night
Je dois promettre de dire bonne nuit à mes parents chaque nuit

They need to recognize the people from France very quickly
Ils ont besoin de reconnaître les gens de France très rapidement

I need to move your cat to another chair
J'ai besoin de déplacer ton chat à une autre chaise

They want to enter the competition and receive a free book
Ils veulent entrer dans la compétition et recevoir un livre gratuit

I see the sun throughout the morning from the kitchen
Je vois le soleil tout au long du matin depuis la cuisine

I go into the house but not through the yard
Je vais dans la maison mais pas par le jardin

*In French the verb "to move" has several definitions. *Déménager* is "to move" to a place while *Déplacer* is "to move" an object, *Bouger* is used in relation to moving a limb or a mechanism.
*With the knowledge you've gained so far, now try to create your own sentences!

To wish	Souhaiter
Bad	Mauvais
To Get	Obtenir
To forget	Oublier
Everybody / Everyone	Tout le monde
Although	Bien que / ça même
To feel	Sentir
Great	Grand
Next	Prochain
To like	Aimer
In front	Devant
Person	Personne
Behind	Derrière
Well	Bien
Goodbye	Au revoir
Restaurant	Restaurant
Bathroom	Les toilettes

I don't want to wish you anything bad
Je ne veux rien te souhaiter de mal
I must forget everybody from my past to feel well
Je dois oublier tout le monde de mon passé pour me sentir bien
I am next to the person behind you
Je suis à côté de la personne derrière toi
There is a great person in front of me
Il y a une grande personne devant moi
I say goodbye to my friends
Je dis au revoir à mes amis
In which part of the restaurant is the bathroom?
Dans quelle partie du restaurant sont les toilettes?
She has to get a car before the next year
Elle besoin d'acheter une voiture avant l'année prochaîne
I want to like the house, but it is very small
Je veux aimer la maison, mais elle est très petite

Tout le monde literally translates into "the entire world," but the actual meaning is "everyone" or "everybody."

To remove	Enlever
Please	S'il vous plaît
Beautiful	Belle / jolie
To lift	Lever
Include / Including	Inclure
Belong	Appartenir
To hold	Tenir
To check	Vérifier
Small	Petit
Real	Vrai / Réel
Week	Semaine
Size	Taille
Even though	Quand même
Doesn't	Pas
So	Alors / Si
Price	Prix

She wants to remove this door please
Elle veut enlever cette porte, s'il vous plaît
This doesn't belong here, I need to check again
Ça n'apartient pas ici, j'ai besoin de vérifier encore
This week the weather was very beautiful
Cette semaine le temps était très beau
I need to know which is the real diamond
J'ai besoin de savoir lequel est le vrai diamant
We need to check the size of the house
Nous avons besoin de vérifier la taille de la maison
I want to lift this, so you need to hold it high
Je veux lever ça, alors tu as besoin de le tenir haut
I can pay this although that the price is expensive
Je peux payer ça même que le prix est élevé
Including everything is this price correct?
Tout inclut c'est le prix correct?

*In French the word *so* has two definitions; *alors* and *si*. *Alors* means *then*, while *si* indicates *so much* or *very*.
- "Then what are we going to see?" / *Alors, qu'est-ce qu'on va voir?*
- "This is so big" / *Cela est si grand*
While *ainsi* and *donc* indicate "thus/therefore" and both can usually be used interchangeably.

BUILDING BRIDGES

In Building Bridges, we take six conjugated verbs that have been selected after studies I have conducted for several months in order to determine which verbs are most commonly conjugated, and which are then automatically followed by an infinitive verb. For example, once you know how to say, "I need," "I want," "I can," and "I like," you will be able to connect words and say almost anything you want more correctly and understandably. The following three pages contain these six conjugated verbs in first, second, third, fourth, and fifth person, as well as some sample sentences. Please master the entire program up until here prior to venturing onto this section.

I want	Je veux
I need	Je besoin
I can	Je peux
I like	J'aime
I go	Je vais
I have	J'ai
I have to /I must	Je dois

Avoir means *to have*, for example: *j'ai un appartement*, "I have an apartment." *Dois* means *to have to* or *must*, for example: *je dois voir*, "I must see."

I want to go to my house
Je veux aller à ma maison
I can go with you to the bus station
Je peux aller avec vous à la station de bus
I need to walk to the muesum
J'ai besoin de marcher au musée
I like to take the train
J'aime prendre le train
I am going to teach a class
Je vais enseigner la classe
I have a book
J'ai un livre
I must speak to my teacher
Je dois parler à mon professeur

Please master pages 16-38, prior to attempting the following two pages!!

You want / do you want	Tu veux / veux – tu
He wants / does he want	Il veut/ Veut-il?
She wants / does she want	Elle veut/ Veut - elle?
We want / do we want	Nous voulons/Voulons – nous?
They want / do they want	Ils / Elles Voulent / Voulent – elles/ ils?
You (plural/ formal sing)	Vous voulez /Voulez - vous?

You need / do you need	Tu as besoin / As – tu besoin?
He needs / does he need	Il a besoin / a –t- il besoin?
She needs / does she need	Elle a besoin / a – t- elle besoin?
We want / do we want	Nous avons besoin / avons – nous besoin?
They need / do they need	Ils/ Elles ont besoin/ ont – ils/ elles besoin?
You (plural/ formal sing)	Vous avez besoin/ Avez – vous besoin?

* In French, the verb " to need" always comes with the verb " to have" (avoir).
In order to make a sentence, the verb "to have" must be conjugated.

You can / can you	Tu peux / Peux – tu?
He can / can he	Il peut / Peut – il?
She can / can she	Elle peut / Peut – elle
We can / can we	Nous pouvons / Pouvons – nous?
They can / can they	Ils / Elles peuvent / Peuvent – ils/elles?
You (plural/ formal sing)	Vous pouvez / Pouvez – vous?

You like / do you like	Tu aimes / Aimes – tu?
He likes / does he like	Il aime / Aime t –il?
She like / does she like	Elle aime / Aime t – elle?
We like / do we like	Nous aimons / Aimons – nous?
They like / do they like	Ils/ elles aiment / Aiment – ils/ elles
You (plural/ formal sing)	Vous aimez / Aimez – vous?

You go / do you go	Tu vas / vas – tu?
He goes / does he go	Il va / Va t – il?
She goes / does she go	Elle va / Va t –elle?
We go / do we go	Nous allons / Allons – nous?
They go / do they go	Ils/ elles vont / vont – ils/ elles?
You (plural/ formal sing)	Vous allez / Allez – vous?

You have / do you have	Tu as / As – tu?
He has / does he have	Il a / A t – il?
She has / does she have	Ell a / A t – elle
We have / do we have	Nous avons / Avons – nous?
They have / do they have	Ils/ elles ont / Ils / elles – ont?
You (plural/ formal sing)	Vous avez / Avez – vous

Questions can be asked by inverting the conjugated verb and the subject pronoun, and then joining them with a hyphen. Example: *Do you want to read? / Veux - tu lire?*

Do you want to go?
Veux- tu aller?
Does he want to fly?
Veut – il prendre l'avion?
We want to swim
Nous voulons nager
Do they want to run?
Veulent-ils courir?
Do you need to clean?
Avez - vous besoin de nettoyer?
As - tu besoin de nettoyer?
She needs to sing a song
Elle besoin chanter une chanson
We need to travel
Nous avons besoin de voyager
They don't need to fight
Ils n'ont pas besoin de se battre
You (plural) need to see
Vous avez besoin de voir
Can you listen to me?
Peux – tu m'écouter?
He can dance very well
Il peut dancer très bien
We can go out tonight
Nous pouvons sortir ce soir
They can break the wood
Ils peuvent casser du bois
Do you like to eat here?
Aimez – vous manger ici
Aime – tu manger ici

He likes to spend time here
Il aime passer du temps ici
We like to fix the house
Nous aimons réparer la maison
They like to cook
Ils aiment cuisiner
You (plural) like my house
Vous aimez ma maison
Do you go to school today?
Allez - vous à l'ecole aujourd'hui?
Vas – tu à l'ecole aujourd'hui
He goes fishing
Il va pêcher
We are going to relax
Nous allons nous détendre
They go to watch a film
Ils vont voir un film
Do you have money?
Avez - vous de l'argent?
As – tu de l'argent?
She must look outside
Elle doit regarder dehors
We have to sign our names
On doit signer avec notre noms
They have to send the letter
Ils / Elles doivent envoyer la lettre
You (plural) have to order
Vous devez commander

BASIC GRAMMATICAL REQUIREMENTS OF THE FRENCH LANGUAGE WHICH YOU WILL ENCOUNTER IN THIS PROGRAM

Feminine and Masculine & Plural and Singular

Every noun in the French language has a masculine or feminine gender. It's crucial to understand a noun's gender since both articles "the" and "a" are altered based on the gender of the noun they are pertaining to. *Le* is the masculine form and *la* is the feminine form of the article "the." The plural form of the *le* and *la* is *les*.

The majority of words that conclude in a constant or a and u are masculine, for example, "the sun" / *le soleil* and "the butterfly" / *le papillon*. French words, ending in *e, é, lle, on, eur, ble, cle, de, ge, me, ste, tre* are considered feminine, for example, "the woman" / *la femme,* "the pool" / *la piscine,* the flower / *la fleur,* and the beach / *la plage.*

Preceding a vowel, the *e* and the *a* from the article *s, la,* and *le* will be automatically eliminated. The article "the" is *l'*, so the (*le*) egg *(oeuf)* is *l'oeuf* and "the actor" is *l'acteur.* Besides the vowels "a," "e," "i," "o," and "u," the letter "h," which is considered silent and isn't a vowel, is occasionally treated according to the same grammar rules as if it was: "the" *(le)* "man" *(homme)* is *l'homme* and "the grass" is *l'herbe.*

In the French language, the feminine form of the words "to the" and "at the" is *à la,* but the masculine form of "to the" is *au.* The same rule applies for *de.* The feminine form is *de la,* but the masculine form is *du.*

Days of the week are not capitalized and are all in masculine form.

Pluralizing nouns

In French, in order to make a noun plural, an *s* must be added. There are a few exceptions though.

If the noun ends with an *eu, ou,* or *er,* add an *x* instead of an *s.* For example, "place" is *lieu.* The plural "places" will be *lieux.* If the noun ends with an *s,* then nothing should be added. For example, my son is *mon fils;* in plural my sons will be *mes fils.* If there is an *al* or *il* at the end of the noun, then replace it with *aux.* For example, "the newspaper" is *il journal;* "the newspapers" is *les journaux.*

Personal Pronouns

In regards to the pronoun "you," there are two ways of saying it in French—*vous* and *tu.*

Vous is the formal "you." Use it when speaking to someone you just met, to authority, or to someone whom you are showing respect. The plural "you" is *vous* as well, and you use it when speaking to a group of people or more than one person.

Tu is the informal "you." Use it when speaking to a friend, acquaintance, relative, or close family member. *Tu* is a subject pronoun (second person of singular), referring to the individual who is doing the action.

Te is a direct and indirect object pronoun, the person who is actually affected by the action that is being carried out. But the *te* comes before the verb: "I need to show you" / *j'ai besoin de te montrer* and "I love you" / *je t'aime.*

Toi is a preposition pronoun, meaning it goes with a preposition: "with you" / *avec toi* and "for you" / *pour toi* and "after you" / *après toi.*

Votre is the formal "your." *Le vôtre* is the formal "yours."

Vos is the plural formal form when referring to several objects: "your cars" / *vos voitures* and "your dogs" / *vos chiens*

Ton is the informal "your." The informal feminine form is *ta.*

Tes is the informal plural form.

Adjectives

In English, adjectives precede the noun, but in French, it's usually the opposite. Fast car will be *voiture rapide,* cold winter will be *hiver froid.*

French adjectives are modified by the number and gender of the nouns which they are pertaining to. Every adjective can have four forms.

- To make a noun masculine, you leave it the way it is.
- To make it feminine, just add an e at the end.
- To make it plural masculine, add an s at the end.
- To make it plural feminine, then simply add es at the end.

For example: smart, intelligent; he is smart will be *il est intelligent,* she is smart *elle est intelligente,* plural masculine, *ils sont intelligents* / plural feminine, *ils sont intelligentes.*

But if the adjective ends with an *s* or *x,* then for masculine plural, add nothing, but for feminine, you must replace the *x* at the end with *se,* and for feminine plural, you replace it with *ses.*

Comparisons

In order to use comparisons add *plus* and *que.*
For example:
Darker than / *Plus sombre que*
Stronger than / *Plus forte que*

Time

When referring to time, *il est une heure* means it's one o'clock. Any number greater than one, the heure becomes pluralized;
il est cinq heures / it's five o'clock, *il est six heures* / it's six o'clock

Verbs

French verbs are conjugated in a different form than English verbs.

To make a verb negative add *ne* before the verb and *pas* after.
For example:
I don't want - *je ne veux pas*
I don't see - *je ne vois pas*
I can't - *je ne peux pas*
I don't like - *je n'aime pas* (since *aime*, "like" begins with a vowel, then the *e* in *ne* is eliminated and it connects to the verb with an apostrophe).
*a contraction is used when the word which follows *ne* begins with a vowel)

Demonstratives

This, ceci and *that, cela* are the formal ways of reference to *this* and *that*. But instead use *ce* and *ça* which are the spoken form. Both **ce** (*cette* feminine tense of *ce* and *ces* is the plural of *ce* and *cette*) and **ça** could mean the same thing; *this, that, and it.*
The difference between the two:
ce- usually goes with a noun, neutral, or the verb *être, to be*
Noun:
that place, ce lieu / that house, cette maison / these days, ces jours
Verb être, to be:
That is a boy, c'est un garçon
That is very easy, c'est très facile
It is not impossible, ce n'est pas impossible
Since *is* is a form of the verb *to be*. *That is or this is (both words connect) ce +est =c'est,* "it's not" or "this/that is not" is "ce n'est".
Neutral:
This idea, cette idée / that journey, ce voyage
Idea and *journey* are neuteral since they can be either male or female.

ça- usually goes with any other verb besides *être;*
I want this, je veux ça / I don't need this, je ne besoin pas ça.

* Both *ce* and *ça* can also be used before the verbs *pouvoir* and *devoir;*
This can be hard, ce peut être difficile/ this must happen, ce doit faire
This can be hard, ça peut être difficile/ this must happen, ça doit faire

OTHER USEFUL TOOLS FOR THE FRENCH LANGUAGE

Reading and Pronunciation

French pronunciation is rather different than English, because there are multiple ways in which letters can become silent. But if you follow these following steps it will help you in French pronuncation.

In general, most consonants in English and French sound the same.

ge and *gi* is pronounced as *je*

h is silent

qu is pronounced as *k*

ch is pronounced as *sh*

th is pronounced as *t*, rather than being pronounced as *th*

Ç and the *r* in the French language are letters which don't exist in English. The *ç* sounds like an *s*.

The French r on the other hand is pronounced at the back of your throat, unlike the *r* in English and Spanish.

Pronouncing Vowels in French
E sounds like "e" in "bed."
É sounds like "ay" as in "day."
Ê, È sounds like "e" in "net."
I, Y sounds like "ee."

Diphthongs
Ail sounds like "i" in "night."
An, en, and *em* are pronounced with a long nasal sound.
Oi sounds like "wa."
Oui sounds like "wee."
O, au, and *eau* sound like the "o" in float."
Ou sounds like "oo" in "pool."
U is pronounced by rounding the mouth like an "o" and saying the letter "e."

Silent letters

The French language has silent letters, which can be divided into three categories:

- E muet / Elision
- H muet and aspiré
- Final consonants

In French, words that end with an *e*, the *e* is usually not pronounced, but the consonant that precedes it will be, for example; *belle* will be pronounced as *bell*, *porte* will be pronounced as *port*. The letter *h* is never pronounced and is silent.

The Elision Rule applies to words ending in *ce, je, me, te, se, de, ne, que,* in which the last letter is omitted, as long as the following word begins with a consonant, and both connect creating one syllable:
I love you, je t'aime
I have, j'ai,
I don't have, je n'ai pas

In the French language the final consonant is dropped. (For example: *Bijoux* will be pronounced as *bijou, tous* will be pronounced as *tou, veux* will be pronounced as *veu*), (except if there is a "*c*", "*f*" and "*l*" which are generally pronounced). In the event a noun or adjective is pluralized the *s* will be dropped as well. For example *cat, chat* will be pronounced as *cha* but in plural *chats* will be pronounced as *chat*. Another example: "*Dans*", meaning "*in*" will be pronounced as *dan* (the "*n*" should not be stressed too strongly). There are a few exceptions though; *avec, club, hiver, avril* and a few others as well.

The Liaison Rule is a situation in which a consonant at the end of a word, which would usually not be pronounced, is pronounced due to the fact that its followed by a word that begins with a vowel or silent *h*, in that situation the *s* or *x* will be pronounced as *z*. *The friends, les amis,* would be pronounced as *lez-amis, deux amis* will be pronounced as *deuz-amis.*

Days of the Week

Sunday	Dimanche
Monday	Lundi
Tuesday	Mardi
Wednesday	Mercredi
Thursday	Jeudi
Friday	Vendredi
Saturday	Samedi

Seasons

Spring	Printemps
Summer	Été
Autumn	Automne
Winter	Hiver

Cardinal Directions

North	Nord
South	Sud
East	Est
West	Ouest

Colors

Black	Noir
White	Blanc
Gray	Gris
Red	Rouge
Blue	Bleu
Yellow	Jaune
Green	Vert
Orange	Orange
Purple	Violet
Brown	Marron

Numbers

One	Un
Two	Deux
Three	Trois
Four	Quatre
Five	Cinq
Six	Six
Seven	Sept
Eight	Huit
Nine	Neuf
Ten	Dix

Conversational
Italian
Quick and Easy

THE MOST INNOVATIVE AND REVOLUTIONARY TECHNIQUE
TO MASTER CONVERSATIONAL ITALIAN

YATIR NITZANY

THE ITALIAN LANGUAGE

The official language of Italy and it has evolved over time, primarily because of the poet Dante Alighieri, who modernized the language by blending the Italian dialects, Sicilian and Tuscan. While the language's Tuscan roots are more prevalent, the now-extinct language, Dalmatian, also inspired Dante. With the combination of these three Romance dialects, the Italian language evolved into its modern state. Spoken by approximately seventy million people, Italian shares the title with Latin as co-official language of the Vatican City, as Italian has Latin roots. Though the language is most widely spoken in Italy, Italian is also spoken in some areas of Switzerland, Croatia, France, Slovenia, and Albania.

Spoken in: Italy

MEMORIZATION MADE EASY

There is no doubt the three hundred and fifty words in my program are the required essentials in order to engage in quick and easy basic conversation in any foreign language. However, some people may experience difficulty in the memorization. For this reason, I created Memorization Made Easy. This memorization technique will make this program so simple and fun that it's unbelievable! I have spread the words over the following twenty pages. Each page contains a vocabulary table of ten to fifteen words. Below every vocabulary box, sentences are composed from the words on the page that you have just studied. This aids greatly in memorization. Once you succeed in memorizing the first page, then proceed to the second page. Upon completion of the second page, go back to the first and review. Then proceed to the third page. After memorizing the third, go back to the first and second and repeat. And so on. As you continue, begin to combine words and create your own sentences in your head. Every time you proceed to the following page, you will notice words from the previous pages will be present in those simple sentences as well, because repetition is one of the most crucial aspects in learning any foreign language. Upon completion of your twenty pages, *congratulations*, you have absorbed the required words and gained a basic, quick-and-easy proficiency and you should now be able to create your own sentences and say anything you wish in the Italian language. This is a crash course in conversational Italian, and it works!

For further assistance in the memorization and pronunciation of the vocabulary of this program, you may also purchase the audio version of this book, which is featured on Amazon, Audible, and iTunes.

Reading and Pronunciation in Italian

Ce - pronounced as "che."
Ci - pronounced as "chi."

When *ci* is followed by a vowel then the *i* drops.

Cia   -   pronounced   as   "cha."
Cie   -   pronounced   as   "che."
Cio   -   pronounced   as   "cho."
Ciu - pronounced as "chu."

Ch - pronounced as "k."
Chi - pronounced as "ki."
Che - pronounced as "ke."
Chi - pronounced as "ki."

Ge - pronounced as "je."
Gi - pronounced as "ji."

When *gi* is followed by a vowel then the *i* drops.
Gia - pronounced as "ja."

Gie - pronounced as "je."
Gio - pronounced as "jo."
Giu - pronounced as "ju."

Gh - before *e* or *i* the *h* drops (*laghi* / "lakes" pronounced as "lagi").
Gli - pronounced as the *lli* in "millions", the *g* is silent.
"I want" / *voglio* - pronounced as "vol-yo."
figlio / "son" - pronounced as "fil-yo."
Gn - the *g* drops and the *n* is pronounced as "ny" (lasagna).

Sce - and *sci* pronounced as "sh."
Sch - before *e* or *i* pronounced as "sk."
When *sci* is followed by a vowel the *i* is dropped.
Scia - pronounced as "sha."

Scie - pronounced as "she."
Scio - pronounced as "sho."
Sciu - pronounced as "shu."

In Italian, when *s* is followed by a vowel and is the second or third or further syllable of the sentence, then it's pronounced as a "z."
Casa is pronounced as "caza."

Z is pronounced as "ts" or "tz."

—It's also important to note that in Italian, whenever encountering double consonants, each letter must be pronounced. *Pizza* is pronounced as "piz-za."
Nonna is pronounced as "non-na."

NOTE TO THE READER

The purpose of this book is merely to enable you to communicate in Italian. In the program itself (pages 16-40) you may notice that the composition of some of those sentences might sound rather clumsy. This is intentional. These sentences were formulated in a specific way to serve two purposes: to facilitate the easy memorization of the vocabulary and to teach you how to combine the words in order to form your own sentences for quick and easy communication, rather than making complete literal sense in the English language. So keep in mind that this is not a phrase book!

As the title suggests, the sole purpose of this program is for conversational use only. It is based on the mirror translation technique. These sentences, as well as the translations are not incorrect, just a little clumsy. Latin languages, Semitic languages, and Anglo-Germanic languages, as well as a few others, are compatible with the mirror translation technique.

Many users say that this method surpasses any other known language learning technique that is currently out there on the market. Just stick with the program and you will achieve wonders!

Again, I wish to stress this program is by no means, shape, or form a phrase book! The sole purpose of this book is to give you a fundamental platform to enable you to connect certain words to become conversational. Please also read the "Introduction" and the "About Me" section prior to commencing the program.

In order to succeed with my method, please start on the very first page of the program and fully master one page at a time prior to proceeding to the next. Otherwise, you will overwhelm yourself and fail. Please do not skip pages, nor start from the middle of the book.

It is a myth that certain people are born with the talent to learn a language, and this book disproves that myth. With this method, anyone can learn a foreign language as long as he or she follows these explicit directions:

* Memorize the vocabulary on each page

* Follow that memorization by using a notecard to cover the words you have just memorized and test yourself.

* Then read the sentences following that are created from the vocabulary bank that you just mastered.

* Once fully memorized, give yourself the green light to proceed to the next page.

Again, if you proceed to the following page without mastering the previous, you are guaranteed to gain nothing from this book. If you follow the prescribed steps, you will realize just how effective and simplistic this method is.

THE PROGRAM

Let's Begin! "Vocabulary"
(Memorize the Vocabulary)

I	I am	Io	Io sono
With you		Con te, con lei / **(Plural)** con voi
With him / with her		Con lui / con lei
With us		Con noi
For you		Per te, per lei / **(Plural)** per voi
Without him		Senza lui
Without them		Senza loro
Always		Sempre
Was		Era
This		Questo
Is		(verb) è / (conjunction) si
Sometimes		A volte / qualche volta
You		(Informal)Te, tu/(formal)Lei/(P)Voi
Are you / you are		**(Temporary)** sei, **(permanent)** siete
Better		Meglio
Today		Oggi
He / She		Lui / Lei
From		Da, di, dall / dalla

Sentences from the vocabulary (now you can speak the sentences and connect the words)

I am with you

Io sono con te

This is for you

Questo è per te

I am from Italy

Sono dall'Italia

Are you from Milan?

Sei di Milano?

Sometimes you are with us at the mall

A volte siete con noi al centro commerciale

I am always with her

Io sono sempre con lei

Are you without them today?

Sei senza di loro oggi?

Sometimes I am with him

A volte io sono con lui

*In Italian, the preposition "from" could be either *da* or *di*. Depending on the case, though, it could be a bit confusing.

*In Italian, the pronoun "you," *te* is the informal and lei is the formal. *Voi* is plural.

I was	Ero
To be	Essere
The	Lo, il, l', gli, i, la, le
Same	Stesso
Good	(Male) Buono / (fem) buona
Here	Qui
It's / it is	è
And	E
Between	Tra
Now	Adesso / ora
Later / After	Più tardi, dopo
If	Se
Yes	Sì
Then	Allora / dopo / poi
Tomorrow	Domani
Very	(M) Molto / (F) molta
Also / too / as well	Anche

Between now and later
Tra adesso e dopo
If it's later, then it is better tomorrow
Se è tardi, allora è meglio domani
This is good as well
Questo è anche buono
Yes, you are very good
Sì, sei molto bravo
I was here with them
Ero qui con loro
You and I
Io e te
The same day
Lo stesso giorno

*In Italian the article "the" has a few different tenses.
-*Lo* — masculine words that start with *gn, pn, ps, x, y, z* (and *s* plus a consonant)
-*Il*—used for any other (masculine) words beginning with consonants, except for *gn,*
pn, ps, x, y, z (and s plus a consonant).
-*L'*—before a vowel or an *h*
-*Gli* —plural form of *lo*
-*I* —the plural form of *il*
-*La* — feminine form
-*Le* —plural form of *la*. Plural remains *le* even if the following word is an *h* or a vowel.

Me	Me
Ok	Ok
Even if	Anche se
Afterwards	Dopo
Worse	Peggio
Where	Dove
Everything	Tutto
Somewhere	De qualche parte
What	Che cosa?
Almost	Quasi /pressapoco
There	Là, lì
Maybe	Forse

Afterwards is worse
Dopo è peggio
Even if I go now
Anche se vado ora
Where is everything?
Dove è tutto?
Maybe somewhere
Forse da qualche parte
What? I am almost there
Che cosa? Sono quasi Là
Where are you?
Dove sei?

*In Italian, pronouns have different tenses.
- "My"—*mio* (male), *mia* (female), *miei* (male plural), *mie* (female plural)
- "Your" (informal)—*tuo* (male), *tua* (female), *tuoi* (m. plural), *tue* (f. plural)
- "Your" (formal)—*vostro* (male), *vostra* (female), *vostri* (m. plural), *vostre* (f. plural)
- "His"/"Her"—suo (male), sua (female), suoi (m. plural), *sue* (f. plural)
- "Our"—*nostro* (male), *nostra* (female), *nostri* (m. plural), *nostre* (f. plural)
- "Their"—*il loro* (male), *la loro* (female), *i loro* (m. plural), *le loro* (f. plural)

House	Casa
In	In
Car	Automobile / macchina
Already	Già
Good morning	Buongiorno
How are you?	Come stai?
Where are you from?	Di dove sei?
But / however	Ma
Hello	Ciao
What is your name?	Come ti chiami?
How old are you?	Quanti anni hai?
Son	Figlio
Daughter	Figlia
At	A
A	(M) uno, un / (F) una
Hard	(*Hard object*) Duro / (*difficult*) difficile
Still	Ancora
Your	Tuo / tua

She is without a car, so maybe she is still at the house?
Lei è senza una macchina, allora forse lei è ancora a casa?
I am in the car already with your son and your daughter
Sono in macchina già con tuo figlio e tua figlia
Good morning, how are you today?
Buon giorno, come stai oggi?
Hello, what is your name?
Ciao, come ti chiami?
How old are you?
Quanti anni hai?
This is very hard, but it's not impossible
Questo è molto difficile, ma non è impossibile
Where are you from?
Di dove sei?

*In Italian, the article "a" has three different tenses.
- Male–*uno* (*gn, j, pn, ps, s* plus consonant, *x, y, z*)
- *Un*—for any other words
- Female–*una*
- *Un'*—before all vowels or *h*—*un'orologio* "a clock"
- Keep in mind *uno* doesn't have this rule concerning vowels and *h*.

Thank you	Grazie
For	Per
Everything	Tutto
This is	Questo è
Time	Ora
But	Ma
No / Not	No
I am not	Io non sono
Away	Lontano
That	(M) questo (F) questa (N) questo
Similar	Simile
Other / Another	Altro
Side	Lato
Until	Fino a
Yesterday	Ieri
Without us	Senza noi
Since	Da
Day	Giorno
Before	Prima

Thanks for everything
Grazie per tutto
It's almost time
E 'quasi ora
I am not here, I am away
Io non sono qui, io sono lontano
That is a similar house
Questa è una casa simile
I am from the other side
Io sono dall'altro lato
But I was here until late yesterday
Ma io ero qui fino a tardi ieri
Since the other day
Dall'altro giorno

*In Italian, *ora* is time, *volte* means (how many) times, and tempo is (length of) time.
*In Italian, the prepositions "of" and "from" could be *di* or *da*. When preceding the article "the," each of these (*di* and *da*) become prefixes and form one character.
di+il=del, di+lo=dello, di+l'=dell', di+la=della, di+i=dei, di+gli=degli, di+le=delle
da +il=dal, da+lo=dallo, da+l'=dall', da+la=dalla, da+i=dai, da+gli=dagli, da+le=dale

I say / I am saying	Dico
What time is it?	Che ora è?
I want	Voglio
Without you	Senza te
Everywhere /wherever	Ovunque / dovunque
I go / I am going	Vado
With	Con
My	(Sing M/F) Mio/mia (Plu) miei
Cousin	(M)Cugino(MP)cugini/(F)cugina(FP)cugine
I need	Ho bisogno
Right now	Adesso / ora
Night	Notte
To see	Vedere
Light	Luce
Outside	Fuori / esterna / esterno
That is	Questo è
Any	Qualsiasi
I see / I am seeing	Vedo

I am saying no / I say no
Dico no / io dico no
I want to see this during the day
Voglio vedere questo durante il giorno
I see this everywhere
Vedo questo ovunque
I am happy without any of my cousins here
Sono felice, senza nessuno dei miei cugini qui
I need to be there at night
Ho bisogno di essere lì durante la notte
I see light outside
Vedo la luce fuori
What time is it right now?
Che ora è adesso?

*In Italian, you aren't required to place a personal pronoun preceding a conjugated verb. For example, "I am saying no" is *dico no* . The word "I" (io) before a conjugated verb isn't required. For example,*io voglio sapere la data* / "I want to know the date" can be said*voglio sapere la data* since*voglio* already means "I want" in the conjugated form, although saying *io* isn't incorrect! The same rule applies to*tu/lui/lei/loro/noi/vostro* —they aren't required to be placed prior to the conjugated verb, but if they are, then it isn't wrong. There are a few exceptions, such as "I need" / *ho bisogno*, "he needs" / *hai bisogno*, etc. "I like" / *mi piace*, again the same rule applies to *tu / lui / lei / loro / noi / vostro* in regards to *piace* and *bisogno*. See page 121 to learn more.

Place	Luogo/ posto
Easy	Facile
To find	Trovare
To look for / to search	Cercare
Near / Close	Vicino / vicina
To wait	Aspettare
To sell	Vendere
To use	Utilizzare / usare
To know	Sapere
To decide	Decidere
That (*conjunction*)	Che
Two	Due
To	A

This place is easy to find
Questo luogo è facile da trovare
I need to look for you next to the car
Ho bisogno di cercarti vicino alla macchina
I am saying to wait until tomorrow
Sto dicendo di aspettare fino a domani
It's easy to sell this table
E 'facile vendere questo tavolo
I want to use this
Voglio usare questo
I need to know where is the house
Ho bisogno di sapere dove si trova la casa
I need to decide between both places
Ho bisogno di decidere tra due luoghi
I need to know that everything is ok
Ho bisogno di sapere che tutto è ok

*In Italian, "I am" has two definitions: *sono* and *sto*. Usually *sono* refers to a more permanent sense. For example, *sono italiano* / "I am Italian" and *sono un uomo* / "I am a man," while *sto* is more of a temporary case. For example, *sto bene* and *sto male*. *Sto* is also used to indicate movement and locations. Although, similar to every language, there are exceptions to the rule such as *sono stanco* / "I am tired." Some of these irregular cases may need to be memorized. Again, this isn't a grammar book.

*This *isn't* a phrase book! The purpose of this book is *solely* to provide you with the tools to create *your own* sentences!

Because	Perché
To buy	Comprare
Both	Entrambi
Them | They	(M) Essi (F) Esse / (M) Loro (F) Loro
Their	La loro
Book / books	Libro / libri
Mine	Mio / mia
To understand	Capire
Problem / Problems	Problema / problemi
I do / I am doing	Faccio / sto facendo
Like this	Così
To look	Guardare
Myself	Io
Each / every	Ogni
Food	Cibo
Water	Acqua
Hotel	Hotel

I like this hotel because I want to look at the beach
Mi piace quest'hotel perché voglio guardare la spiaggia
I want to buy a bottle of water
Voglio comprare una bottiglia d'acqua
I do it like this each day
Io faccio questo così ogni giorno
Both of them have enough food
Entrambi hanno cibo a sufficienza
This is the book, and this book is mine
Questo è il libro, e questo libro è mio
I need to understand the problem
Ho bisogno di capire il problema
From the hotel I have a view of the city
Dall'hotel ho una vista della città
I can work today
Posso lavorare oggi
I do my homework
Faccio i miei compiti

*In Italian, male nouns end in o; usually their plural form ends with an i. Female nouns end in *a;* usually their plural form ends with an e. For example, "boy" / *ragazzo,* "boys" / *ragazzi,* "girl" / *ragazza,* "girls" / *ragazze.* Female nouns that end in ea, when pluralized, become *ee.* Female nouns ending in ca, their plural form ends in *che.* Nouns ending with an e usually will end with an i when pluralized. Words of foreign origin when pluralized will stay the same, for example, "the motel" / *il motel* and "the motels" / *i motel.*

105

I like	Mi piace
There is / There are	C'è / ci sono
Family / Parents	Famiglia / Genitori
Why	Perché
To say	Dire
Something	Qualcosa
To go	Andare
Ready	Pronto
Soon	Presto
To work	Lavorare
Who	Chi
To stay	Stare

I like to stay at my house with my parents
Mi piace stare a casa mia con miei genitori
I want to know why?
Voglio sapere perché
Do I need to say something important?
Ho bisogno dire qualcosa importante?
I am there with him
sono là con lui
I am busy, but I need to be ready soon
Io sono impegnato, ma ho bisogno di essere pronto presto
I like to go to work
Mi piace andare a lavorare
Who is there?
Chi è là?
I want to know if they are here, because I want to go outside
Voglio sapere se sono qui, perché voglio andare fuori
There are seven dolls
Ci sono sette bambole

*In Italian, "I need" is *ho bisogno,* and "do I need" is *ho bisogno* as well. Please see page 121 to learn more.

*In Italian, the verb like / *piace* changes to *piacciono* whenever the noun is pluralized. For example, "I like the house" is *mi piace la casa.* However, "I like the houses" is mi *piacciono le case.* The same rule applies to other possessive adjectives as well: *ti piacciono, le piacciono, gli piacciono, vi piacciono,* and *piacciono a loro.*

How much	Quanto
To bring	Portare
With me	Con mei
Instead	Invece
Only	Solo / soltano
When	Quando
I can / Can I?	Posso / posso?
Or	O
Were	Erano
Without me	Senza me
Fast	Veloce
Slow	Lento, lentamente, piano
Cold	Freddo
Inside	Interno
To eat	Mangiare
Hot	Caldo
To Drive	Guidare

How much money do I need to bring with me?
Quanti soldi devo portare con me?
Instead of this cake, I like that cake
Invece di questa torta mi piace quella torta
Only when you can
Solo quando tu puoi
They were without me yesterday
Erano senza di me ieri
I need to drive the car very fast or very slowly
Ho bisogno di guidare la macchina molto veloce o molto lentamente
It is cold inside the library
Fa freddo all'interno della libreria
Yes, I like to eat this hot for my lunch
Sì, mi piace mangiare questa calda per il mio pranzo

To answer	Rispondere
To fly	Volare
I must	Devo
To travel	Viaggiare
To learn	Imparare
How	Come
To swim	Nuotare
To practice	Practicare
To play	Giocare
To leave	Lasciare
Many/much /a lot	(M)Molto (F)Molta
I go to	Vado a
First	Prima
Time / Times	Volta / volte

I need to answer many questions
Ho bisogno di rispondere a molte domande
The bird must fly
L'uccello deve volare
I need to learn to swim at the pool
Ho bisogno di imparare nuotare in piscina
I want to learn everything about how to play better tennis
Voglio imparare tutto su come giocare meglio a tennis
I want to leave this here for you when I go to travel the world
Voglio lasciare questo qui per te quando vado a viaggiare per il mondo
Since the first time
Dalla prima volta
The children are yours
I bambini sono tuoi

*In Italian, "many," "much," and "a lot" is *molto* (m), *molti* (m. plur.), *molta* (f), and *molte* (f. plur.).
*With the knowledge you've gained so far, now try to create your own sentences!

Nobody / Anyone	Nessuno /chiunque
Against	Contro
Us	Noi
To visit	Visitare
Mom / Mother	Mamma
To give	Dare
Which	Quale
To meet	Incontrare
Someone	Qualcuno
Just	Soltanto
To walk	Camminare
Around	Intorno
Towards	Verso
Than	Che / di
Nothing	Niente

Something is better than nothing

Qualcosa è meglio di niente

I am against him

Io sono contro di lui

We go to visit my family each week

Andiamo a visitare la mia famiglia ogni settimana

I need to give you something

Ho bisogno darti qualcosa

Do you want to meet someone

Vuoi incontrare qualcuno?

I am here on Wednesdays as well

Sono qui anche il mercoledì

You do this everyday?

Tu fai questo tutti i giorni?

*In Italian the pronoun "you" has three different definitions: *tu, ti,* and *te.*
Tu is the subject pronoun "you" (informal), for example, *tu vuoi* / "do you want."
Ti is an object pronoun, for example, *ti mostro come* / "I show you how." In Italian, we use *ti* when someone is doing something "to you" or "at you." *Ti* is a direct and indirect object pronoun, the person who is actually affected by the action that is being carried out. But the *ti* comes before the conjugated verb. For example, "I send you" is *ti mando* and "I permit you" is ti *permetto.* In the event the verb is in the infinitive form, the ti follows the verb and connects to the end as a suffix, and you must also remove the e at the end of that verb:
- "to give" / *dare*
- "to give you" / *darti*
Te is used after a verb (*ho bisogno te* / "I need you") as a prepositional pronoun, meaning it goes with a preposition (like *per te*).

I have	Ho
Don't	Non
Friend	(**Male**)Amico /(**female**)amica
To borrow	Prendere in prestito
To look like	Apparire
Grandfather	Nonno
To want	Volere
Wrong / incorrect	Scorretto
To continue	Continuare
Way	(*path*)Via / (*method*) maniera
That's why	Quindi
To show	Mostrare
To prepare	Preparare
I am not going	Non vado

Do you want to look like Arnold?
Vuoi apparire come Arnold?
I want to borrow this book for my grandfather
Voglio prendere in prestito questo libro per mio nonno
I want to drive and to continue on this way to my house
Voglio guidare e continuare per questa via a casa mia
I have a friend, that's why I want to stay in Rome
Ho un amico, per questo voglio stare a Roma
I am not going to see anyone here
Non vedo nessuno qui
I need to show you how to prepare breakfast
Ho bisogno di mostrarti come preparare la colazione
Why don't you have the book?
Perché non hai il libro?
That is incorrect, I don't need the car today
Questo è scorretto, non ho bisogno la macchina oggi

To remember	Ricordare
About (*on*)	Su
About (*proximity*)	Circa
Number	Numero
Hour	Ora
Dark / darkness	Scuro / oscurità
Grandmother	Nonna
Five	Cinque
Minute / Minutes	Minuto / Minuti
More	Più
To think	Pensare
To do	Fare
To come	Venire
To hear	Sentire
Last	(M)Ultimo /(F)Ultima

You must remember my number
Tu devi ricordare il mio numero
This is the last hour of darkness
Questa è l'ultima ora delle sera
I want to come and to hear my grandmother speak Italian today
Voglio venire e sentire la mia nonna parlare oggi italiano
I need to think more about this, and what to do
Ho bisogno di pensare di più su questo, e di che cosa fare
From here until there, it's only five minutes
Da qui fino a lì, è a soli cinque minuti

We	Noi
To leave (*a place*)	Andare
To leave (*something*)	Lasciare
Again	Ancora
Italy	Italia
To take	Prendere
To try	Provare
To rent	Affittare
Without her	Senza lei
We are	Siamo
To turn off	Spegnere
To ask	Chiedere
To stop	Fermare
Permission	Permesso / autorizzazione

He needs to leave and rent a house at the beach
Ha bisogno di andare e affittare una casa al mare
I want to pass the test without her
Voglio passare il test senza di lei
We are here a long time
Siamo qui da molto tempo
I need to turn off the lights early tonight
Ho bisogno spegnere le luci presto stasera
We want to stop here
Noi vogliamo fermarci qui
We came from Sicily
Siamo venuti dalla Sicilia
The same building
Lo stesso edificio
I want to ask permission to go
Voglio chiedere il permesso di andare

*In Italian, *molto* can mean "very" and it can mean "long."

To open	Aprire
To buy	Comprare
To pay	Pagare
On	Su
Without	Senza
Sister	Sorella
To hope	Sperare
To live	Vivere
Nice to meet you	Piacere di conoscerti
Name	Nome
Last name	Cognome
To return	Tornare
Our	Nostro
Door	Porta

I need to open the door for my sister
Ho bisogno di aprire la porta per mia sorella
I need to buy something
Ho bisogno di comprare qualche cosa
I want to meet your sisters
Voglio conoscere le tue sorelle
Nice to meet you, what is your name and your last name?
Piacere di conoscerti, come ti chiami e il tuo cognome?
(Formal) Piacere di conoscerla, come si chiami e il suo cognome?
To hope for the better in the future
Sperare il meglio per il futuro
I want to return from the United States and to live without problems in Italy
Voglio tornare dagli Stati Uniti e vivere in Italia senza avere problemi
Why are you sad right now?
Perche' sei triste adesso?
This is our house on the hill
Questa e la nostra casa sulla colina

*When the preposition "on" is followed by the article "the," they form a suffix:
- on the hill / *sua + la colina = sulla colina.*
Depending on each case, the suffix changes:
- *su + il = sul, su + lo = su*
- *su + la = sulla, su + i = sui*
- *su + gli = sugli, su + le = sulle*
*Avere means "to have."

To happen	Accadere
To order	Ordinare
To drink	Bere
Excuse me	Scusi
Child	(M)Bambino/ (F)bambina
Woman	Donna
To begin / To start	Iniziare
To finish	Finire
To help	Aiutare
To smoke	Fumare
To love	Amare
To talk / To Speak	Parlare

This must happen today
Questo deve accadere oggi
Excuse me, my child is here as well
Scusami, il mio bambino è anche qui
I love you
Ti amo
I see you
Ti vedo
I need you
Ho bisogno di te
I need to begin soon to be able to finish at 3 o'clock in the afternoon
Ho bisogno di iniziare presto per essere in grado di finire alle 3 del pomeriggio
I want to help
Voglio aiutare
I don't want to smoke again
Non voglio fumare di nuovo
I want to learn to speak Italian
Voglio imparare a parlare italiano

*In Italian, the possessive adjectives are always preceded by the article "the."
- *"my"—il mio, la mia, i miei, le mie*
- *"his" and "her"—il suo, la sua, i suoi, le sue*
The same rule applies to other possessive adjectives as well.
*In Italian, there are two cases for the verb "can" / "to be able to." *Posso* is the first person conjugated form of the infinitive verb potere, which means "being allowed" to do something. "Can I go?" / *posso andare? Grado* is the first person conjugated form of the infinitive verb *riuscire,* which means "to succeed." "I can" / "am able to do this" / *io sono in grado di fare questo.*

To read	Leggere
To write	Scrivere
To teach	Insegnare
To close	Chiudere
To turn on	Accendere
To prefer	Preferire
To put	Mettere
Less	Meno
Sun	Sole
Month / months	Mese / messi
I Talk	Parlo
Exact	Esatto
To choose	Scegliere

I need this book to learn how to read and write in Italian because I want to teach in Italy
Ho bisogno di questo libro per imparare a leggere e scrivere in Italiano perché voglio insegnare in Italia
I want to close the door of the house and not to turn on the light
Voglio chiudere la porta della casa e non accendere la luce
I prefer to put the gift here
Io preferisco mettere il regalo qui
I want to pay less than you for the dinner
Io voglio pagare meno che tu per la cena
I speak with the boy and the girl in Italian
Parlo con il ragazzo e la ragazza in italiano
There is sun outside today
C'è sole fuori oggi
Is it possible to know the exact date?
E' possibile sapere la data esatta?
I need to go to sleep now in order to wake up early so I can take a taxi to the airport
Ho bisogno di dormirme ora, per svegliarme prima per prendere un taxi al'aeroporto.

*With the knowledge you've gained so far, now try to create your own sentences!

To exchange	Scambiare
To call	Chiamare
Brother	Fratello
Dad	Papà
To sit	Sedersi
Together	Insieme
To change	Cambiare
Of course	Certo
Welcome	Benvenuto
During	Durante
Years	Anno/anni
Sky	Cielo
Up	Su
Down	Giù
Sorry	Dispiace
To follow	Seguire
Her	Lei
Big	Grande
New	Nuovo
Never	Mai

I don't want to exchange this money at the bank
Non voglio scambiare il denaro in banca
I want to call my brother and my dad today
Voglio chiamare mio fratello e mio padre oggi
Of course I can come to the theater, and I want to sit together with you and with your sister
Certo posso venire a teatro, e voglio sedermi insieme con te e con tua sorella
I need to go down to see your new house
Ho bisogno di andare giù per vedere la vostra nuova casa
I can see the sky from the window
Posso vedere il cielo dalla finestra
I am sorry, but he wants to follow her to the store
Mi dispiace, ma vuole seguirla al negozio
It never rains
Non piova mai

To allow	Consentire
To believe	Credere
Morning	Mattina
Except	Tranne
To promise	Promettere
Good night	Buona notte
To recognize	Riconoscere
People	Gente
To move	Spostare
Far	Lontano
Different	Differente / diverso
Man	Uomo
To enter	Entrare
To receive	Ricevere
Throughout	Durante
Good afternoon	Buon pomeriggio
Through	Attraverso
Him / Her	Lui / lei

I need to allow him to go with us, he is a different man now
Ho bisogno di permettergli di andare con noi, lui è un uomo diverso ora
I believe everything, except for this
Credo tutto, tranne questo
I must promise to say good night to my parents each night
Devo promettere di dire la buona notte ai miei genitori ogni notte
They need to recognize the people from Italy very quickly
Hanno bisogno di riconoscere le persone dal'Italia molto velocemente
I need to move your cat to another chair
Ho bisogno di spostare il vostro gatto a un'altra sedia
They want to enter the competition and receive a free book
Vogliono partecipare al concorso e ricevere un libro gratuito
I see the sun throughout the morning from the kitchen
Vedo il sole durante la mattina dalla cucina
I go into the house but not through the yard
Vado in casa, ma non attraverso il cortile

---

*In Italian we use *a* to indicate "to". However the plural case of "to" is *ai*.

To wish	Augurare
Bad	Cattivo
To Get	Ottenere
To forget	Dimenticare
Everybody / Everyone	Tutti
Although	Anche se
To feel	Sentire
Great	Grande
Next	Prossimo
To like	Piacere
In front	Di fronte
Person	Dietro
Behind	Persona
Well	Bene
Goodbye	Arrivederci
Restaurant	Ristorante
Bathroom	Bagno

I don't want to wish you anything bad
Non voglio augurarti nulla di male
I must forget everybody from my past in order to feel well
Devo dimenticarmi di tutti dal mio passato per sentirmi bene
I am next to the person behind you
Sono accanto alla persona dietro di te
There is a great person in front of me
C'e una bella persona di fronte a me
I say goodbye to my friends
Dico arrivederci ai mie amici
In which part of the restaurant is the bathroom?
In quale parte del ristorante e' il bagno?
She has to get a car before the next year
Lei deve prendere una automobile prima del prossimo anno
I want to like the house, but it is very small
Voglio che la casa mi piaccia, ma e' molto piccola

To remove	Rimuovere
Please	Per favore
Beautiful	Bello / bella
To lift	Sollevare
Include / Including	Compreso
Belong	Appartenere
To hold	Tenere
To check	Verificare
Small	Piccolo
Real	Vero
Week	Settimana
Size	Misura
Even though	Anche se
Doesn't	Non
So	Così (*thus*) / tanto (*so much*)
Price	Prezzo

She wants to remove this door please
Vuole rimuovere questa porta per favore
This doesn't belong here, I need to check again
Questo non appartiene qui, ho bisogno di verificare di nuovo
This week the weather was very beautiful
Questa settimana il tempo era molto bello
I need to know which is the real diamond
Ho bisogno di sapere qual'è il vero diamante
We need to check the size of the house
Abbiamo bisogno di controllare la dimensione della casa
I want to lift this, that's why you need to hold it high
Voglio alzare questo, quindi è necessario tenerlo alto
I can pay this although that the price is expensive
Posso pagare questo, anche se il prezzo è caro
Including everything is this price correct?
Tutto incluso è il prezzo corretto?

BUILDING BRIDGES

In Building Bridges, we take six conjugated verbs that have been selected after studies I have conducted for several months in order to determine which verbs are most commonly conjugated, and which are then automatically followed by an infinitive verb. For example, once you know how to say, "I need," "I want," "I can," and "I like," you will be able to connect words and say almost anything you want more correctly and understandably. The following three pages contain these six conjugated verbs in first, second, third, fourth, and fifth person, as well as some sample sentences. Please master the entire program up until here prior to venturing onto this section.

I want	Voglio
I need	Ho bisogno
I can	Posso
I like	Mi piace
I go	Vado
I have to /I must	Devo

I want to go to my house
Voglio andare a casa mia
I can go with you to the bus station
Posso venire con te alla stazione degli autobus
I need to walk to the museum
Ho bisogno di camminare al museo
I like to take the train
Mi piace prendere il treno
I have to speak to my teacher
Devo parlare con il mio insegnante

Please master pages 16-38, prior to attempting the following two pages!!

You want / do you want? - Vuoi / vuoi?
He wants / does he want? - Vuole / vuole?
She wants / does she want? - Vuole / vuole?
We want / do we want? - Vogliamo / vogliamo?
They want / do they want? - Vogliono / vogliono?
You (plural/ formal sing) - Voi volete / voi volete?

You need / do you need? - Hai bisogno / hai bisogno?
He needs / does he need? - Ha bisogno/ ha bisogno?
She needs / does she need? - Ha bisogno / ha bisogno?
We need / do we need? - Abbiamo bisogno / abbiamo bisogno?
They need / do they need? - Hanno bisogno / cosa hanno bisogno?
You (plural/ formal sing) - Voi avete bisogno / voi avete bisogno?

You can / can you? - Puoi / puoi?
He can / can he? - Può / può?
She can / can she? - Può / può?
We can / can we? - Possiamo / possiamo?
They can / can they? - Possono / possono?
You (plural/ formal sing) - Potete/ potete?

You like / do you like? - Ti piace / ti piace ?
He likes / does he like? - Lui piace / lui piace?
She like / does she like? - Lei piace / lei piace?
We like / do we like? - Noi piace / noi piace?
They like / do they like? - A loro piace / a loro piace?
You (plural/ formal sing) - Vi piace / vi piace?

You go / do you go? - Va / vai?
He goes / does he go? - Va / va?
She goes / does she go? - Va / va?
We go / do we go? - Andiamo / andiamo?
They go / do they go? - Vanno / vanno?
You (plural/ formal sing) - Vanno / vanno?

You have / do you have? - Hai / hai?
He has / does he have? - Ha / ha?
She has / does she have? - Ha / ha?
We have / do we have? - Abbiamo / abbiamo?
They have / do they have? - Hanno / hanno?
You (plural/ formal sing) - Hanno / hanno?

You must /must you? - Devi / devi?
He must /must he? - Deve / deve?
She must / must she? - Deve / deve?
We must /must we? - Dobbiamo / dobbiamo?
They must /must they? - Devono / devono?
You (plural) - Devono / devono?

Please master pages 16-38, prior to attempting this pages!!

Do you want to go?
Vuoi andare?
Does he want to fly?
Vuole volare?
We want to swim
Vogliamo nuotare
Do they want to run?
Vogliono correre?
Do you need to clean?
Hai bisogno di pulire?
She needs to sing a song
Ha bisogno di cantare una canzone
We need to travel
Abbiamo bisogno di viaggiare
They don't need to fight
Non hanno bisogno di lottare
You (plural) need to see
Hanno bisogno di vedere
Can you hear me?
Puoi sentirmi?
Yes, he can dance very well
Si, può ballare molto bene
We can go out tonight
Possiamo uscire stasera
They can break the wood
Loro possono rompere il legno
Do you like to eat here?
Ti piace mangiare qui?

He likes to spend time here
A lui piace trascorrere del tempo qui
We like to fix the house
A noi piace sistemare la casa
They like to cook
A loro piace cucinare
You (plural) like my house
A loro piace la mia casa
Do you go to school today?
Vai a scuola oggi?
He goes fishing
Lui va a pescare
We are going to relax
Stiamo andando a rilassarsi
They go to watch a film
Vanno a guardare un film
Do you have money?
Hai soldi?
She must look outside
Lei deve guardare fuori
We have to sign our names
Dobbiamo firmare i nostri nomi
They have to send the letter
Devono inviare la lettera
You (plural) have to order
Devono ordinare

Other Useful Tools in Italian

Days of the Week

Sunday	Domenica
Monday	Lunedi
Tuesday	Martedì
Wednesday	Mercoledì
Thursday	Giovedi
Friday	Venerdì
Saturday	Sabato

Seasons

Spring	Primavera
Summer	Estate
Autumn	Autunno
Winter	Inverno

Colors

Black	Nero
White	Bianco
Gray	Grigio
Red	Rosso
Blue	Blu
Yellow	Giallo
Green	Verde
Orange	Arancione
Purple	Viola
Brown	Marrone

Numbers

One	Uno
Two	Due
Three	Tre
Four	Quattro
Five	Cinque
Six	Sei
Seven	Sette
Eight	Otto
Nine	Nove
Ten	Dieci

Cardinal Directions

North	Nord
South	Sud
East	Est
West	Ovest

Conversational
Portuguese
Quick and Easy

YATIR NITZANY

THE PORTUGUESE LANGUAGE

Portuguese has over 200 million native speakers, and it is the sixth most common language in the world. The language originated from Latin roots and became popular after a Roman invasion of the western region of the Iberian Peninsula (the area known today as Portugal) during the third century BC. The incoming Romans blended their language with that of the natives, so Portuguese began to change. Traders of the time began to use the language, so it spread rapidly, making its way into Africa and Asia and eventually Brazil. In fact, before the language was officially modernized, it was quite unique. Today, there are more traces of Greek and Latin and fewer words from the original Portuguese language.

Spoken in: Portugal, Brazil, Angola, Mozambique, Guinea-Bissau, Cape Verde, and São Tomé and Príncipe

MEMORIZATION MADE EASY

There is no doubt the three hundred and fifty words in my program are the required essentials in order to engage in quick and easy basic conversation in any foreign language. However, some people may experience difficulty in the memorization. For this reason, I created Memorization Made Easy. This memorization technique will make this program so simple and fun that it's unbelievable! I have spread the words over the following twenty pages. Each page contains a vocabulary table of ten to fifteen words. Below every vocabulary box, sentences are composed from the words on the page that you have just studied. This aids greatly in memorization. Once you succeed in memorizing the first page, then proceed to the second page. Upon completion of the second page, go back to the first and review. Then proceed to the third page. After memorizing the third, go back to the first and second and repeat. And so on. As you continue, begin to combine words and create your own sentences in your head. Every time you proceed to the following page, you will notice words from the previous pages will be present in those simple sentences as well, because repetition is one of the most crucial aspects in learning any foreign language. Upon completion of your twenty pages, congratulations, you have absorbed the required words and gained a basic, quick-and-easy proficiency and you should now be able to create your own sentences and say anything you wish in Portuguese. This is a crash course in conversational Portuguese, and it works!

For further assistance in the memorization and the pronunciation of the vocabulary of this program, you may also purchase the audio version of this book, which is featured on Amazon, Audible, and iTunes.

NOTE TO THE READER

The purpose of this book is merely to enable you to communicate in Portuguese. In the program itself (pages 16-40) you may notice that the composition of some of those sentences might sound rather clumsy. This is intentional. These sentences were formulated in a specific way to serve two purposes: to facilitate the easy memorization of the vocabulary and to teach you how to combine the words in order to form your own sentences for quick and easy communication, rather than making complete literal sense in the English language. So keep in mind that this is not a phrase book!

As the title suggests, the sole purpose of this program is for conversational use only. It is based on the mirror translation technique. These sentences, as well as the translations are not incorrect, just a little clumsy. Latin languages, Semitic languages, and Anglo-Germanic languages, as well as a few others, are compatible with the mirror translation technique.

Many users say that this method surpasses any other known language learning technique that is currently out there on the market. Just stick with the program and you will achieve wonders!

Again, I wish to stress this program is by no means, shape, or form a phrase book! The sole purpose of this book is to give you a fundamental platform to enable you to connect certain words to become conversational. Please also read the "Introduction" and the "About Me" section prior to commencing the program.

In order to succeed with my method, please start on the very first page of the program and fully master one page at a time prior to proceeding to the next. Otherwise, you will overwhelm yourself and fail. Please do not skip pages, nor start from the middle of the book.

It is a myth that certain people are born with the talent to learn a language, and this book disproves that myth. With this method, anyone can learn a foreign language as long as he or she follows these explicit directions:

* Memorize the vocabulary on each page

* Follow that memorization by using a notecard to cover the words you have just memorized and test yourself.

* Then read the sentences following that are created from the vocabulary bank that you just mastered.

* Once fully memorized, give yourself the green light to proceed to the next page.

Again, if you proceed to the following page without mastering the previous, you are guaranteed to gain nothing from this book. If you follow the prescribed steps, you will realize just how effective and simplistic this method is.

THE PROGRAM

Let's Begin! "Vocabulary" (Memorize the Vocabulary)

I	Eu
With you	Contigo
With him / wih her	Com Ele / Com Ela
With us	Conosco
For you	Para você
Without him	Sem ele
Without them	(Masc)Sem Eles / (Fem)Sem elas
Always	Sempre
Was	Estive / fui
This	Isto
Is	Está / É
Sometimes	Algumas Vezes
Maybe	Talvez
Are you	Você está / você é
Better	Melhor
I am	Eu sou / Estou
He / She , her	Ele / Ela
From	De / Do

Sentences composed from the vocabulary (now you can speak the sentences and combine the words).

I am with you
Estou contigo

Sometimes I am with him
Algumas vezes estou com ele

Are you without them today?
Você está sem eles hoje?

Sometimes you are with us at the mall
Algumas vezes você está conosco o mall

This is for you
Isto e para você

I am always with her
Estou sempre com ela

I am from Manaus
Eu sou de Manaus

Are you from Brazil?
Você é do Brasil?

Concerning eu sou,estou / é,esta & você está,você é please refer to the permanent and temporary section on page #159.

*Please also see page #163, in order to gain proficiency in the reading and pronunciation, of the Portuguese language.

I was	Estive / fui
To be	Estar / Ser
The	O / A / Os / As
Same	Mesmo / Igual
Good	(M)Bom / (F)boa
Here	Aqui
It's	Está / É
And	E
Between	Entre
Now	Agora
Later / After	Depois
If	Se
Yes	Sim
Then	Então
Tomorrow	Amanhã
You	Você / Tu / **(Plural)** Vocês
Also / too / as well	Também

Between now and later
Entre agora e depois
If it's later, then it's better tomorrow
Se está tarde, então é melhor amanhã
This is good as well
Isto é bom também
To be the same
Estar igual
Yes, you are very good
Sim, você e muito bom
I was here with them
Eu estive aqui com eles
You and I
Você e eu
The same day
O mesmo dia

*Concerning *o,as,os & as* please refer to the *singular and plural* section on page #158.
*Concerning *estar,ser* please refer to the *permanent and temporary* section on page #159.

Me	Me / mim
Ok	Ok
Even if	Inclusive
Afterwards	Depois
Worse	Pior
Where	Onde
Everything	Tudo
Somewhere	Algum lugar
What	Que
Almost	Quase
There	Lá / Ali

Afterwards is worse
Depois é pior
Even if I go now
Inclusive eu vou agora
Where is everything?
Onde está tudo?
Maybe somewhere
Talvez em algum lugar
What? I am almost there
Que? Estou quase lá
Where are you?
Onde está você?

House / Home	Casa / Lar
In	Em / Dentro
Car	Auto / Carro
Already	Já
Good morning	Bom dia
How are you?	Como está você?
Where are you from?	De onde você é?
Today	Hoje
Hello	Alô / Olá / Oi
What is your name?	Qual é o seu nome?
How old are you?	Quantos anos você tem?
Son	Filho
Daughter	Filha
At	Em / (M)No / (F)Na
Very	Muito
Hard	Difícil / Duro
Without us	Sem nós

She is without a car, so maybe she is still at the house?
Ela está sem um carro, talvez ela está ainda em casa
I am in the car already with your son and daughter
Eu já estou no carro com teu filho e filha
Good morning, how are you today?
Bom dia, como está você hoje?
Hello, what is your name?
Oi, qual é seu nome?
How old are you?
Quantos anos você tem?
This is very hard, but it's not impossible
Isto é muito difícil, mas não é impossível
Where are you from?
De onde é você ?

*In Portuguese, "it's not" is flipped around and becomes *não é* or *não esta*.
*In Portuguese, in regards to the pronoun "your," there are two ways of saying it—*tua or seu (male), sua (female)*. *Tua* is the informal "your." Use it when speaking to a friend or someone whom you know well, while *seu* and *sua* are the formal "your;" use them when speaking to an authority, professor, someone whom you just met, or someone to whom you show respect.

Thank you	(M)Obrigado / (F)Obrigada
For / In order to	Para
Anything	Qualquer coisa / Tudo
It's	é / Isto é
Time	Tempo
But	Mas
No / Not	Não
I am not	Eu não estou / Eu não sou
Away	Longe / Distante
That	(M) Este, (F) Esta
Similar	Similar / Parecido
Other / Another	Outro / Um outro
Side	Lado
Until	Até
Yesterday	Ontem
Still	Ainda / Todavia
Since	Desde
Day	Dia
Before	Antes

Thanks for anything
Obrigado por tudo
It's almost time
É quase tempo
I am not here, I am away.
Eu não estou aqui, estou longe.
That is a similar house
Esta é uma casa parecida
I am from the other side
Estou do outro lado
But I was here until late yesterday
Mas eu estive aqui até tarde da noite de ontem
Since the other day
Desde o outro dia

I say / I am saying	Eu digo / Estou dizendo
What time is it?	Que horas são?
I want	Quero
Without you	Sem você
Everywhere	Em todo Lugar
I go / I am going	Eu vou / Estou indo
With	Com
My	(S)(M/F)Meu/Minha (P)(M/F)Meus/Minhas
Cousin	Primo
I need	Preciso
Right now	Neste momento
Night	Noite
To see	Ver
Light	Luz
Outside	Fora
That is	Isto é
Any	Qualquer
I see / I am seeing	Eu vejo / Estou vendo

I am saying no / I say no
Estou dizendo não / Eu digo não
I want to see this during the day
Eu quero ver isto durante o dia
I see this everywhere
Eu vejo isso em todos os lugares
I am happy without my cousins here
Estou feliz sem os meus primos aqui
I need to be there at night
Preciso estar lá à noite
I see light outside
Eu vejo luz lá fora
What time is it right now?
Que horas são agora?

*In Portuguese, placing the pronoun "I" / *eu* before a conjugated verb isn't required. For example, "I want to use this" is *quero usar isto* instead of *eu quero usar isto,* although saying *eu quero usar* isn't incorrect. The same rule also applies for the pronouns "you," "he," "she," "them," and "we." Read page 160 to learn more.
*This *isn't* a phrase book! The purpose of this book is *solely* to provide you with the tools to create *your own* sentences!

Place	Lugar
Easy	Fácil
To find	Encontrar
To look for/ To search	Procurar /Buscar
Near	Perto
To wait	Esperar
To sell	Vender
To use	Usar
To know	Saber
To decide	Decidir
Between	Entre
Both	Ambos / os dois
To	De

This place is easy to find
Este lugar e muito fácil de encotrar
I need to look for you next to the car
Eu preciso procurar por você próximo do carro
I am saying to wait until tomorrow
Eu estou dizendo para esperar até amanhã
It's easy to sell this table
É fácil vender esta mesa
I want to use this
Eu quero usar isto
I need to know where is the house
Eu preciso saber onde está a casa
I need to decide between the two places
Eu preciso decidir entre os dois lugares
I am very happy to know that everything is ok
Estou muito feliz em saber que tudo está bem

*In English, an infinitive verb is always preceded by "to": "to want," "to wait," "to decide." But in Portuguese and Spanish, the *ar, er,* or *ir* at the end of the verb makes it infinitive: *querer, esperar, decidir.* Occasionally you can place a *para* preceding the infinitive verb: "to wait" / *para esperar.*

*"That" / "which" can also be used as relative pronouns. The translation in Portuguese is *que.* "I am very happy to know that everything is ok" / *estou muito feliz em saber que tudo está bem.*

Because	Porque
To buy	Comprar
Like this	Asi
Them | They	(M) Eles / (F) Elas
I can / Can I	Eu Posso / Posso?
Book	Livro
Mine	Meu
To understand	Entender / Compreender
Problem / Problems	Problema / Problemas
I do / I am doing	Eu faço / Eu estou fazendo
Of	(S)(M/F)Do/Da (P)(M/F)Dos,Das (N)De
To look	Olhar
Myself	Eu mesmo
Enough	Bastante
Food	Comida
Water	Agua
Hotel	Hotel

I like this hotel because I want to look at the beach
Eu gosto deste hotel porque eu quero olhar a praia
I want to buy a bottle of water
Eu quero comprar uma garrafa de água
Both of them have enough food
Ambos deles tem bastante comida
That is the book, and that book is mine
Isto é um livro, e este livro é meu
I need to understand the problem
Eu preciso entender o problema
I see the view of the city from the hotel
Eu vejo a vista da cidade do hotel
I can work today
Eu posso trabalhar hoje
I do my homework
Eu faço meu dever de casa

*In the Portuguese language, certain words connect to form one word. For example:
- de (of) + eles (them) = deles
- de (of) + este (this) = deste
To learn more about these connections, please refer to page 161.
*To learn more about the conjugation of "of," please refer to
158 & 161 to learn more.

I like	Eu gosto
There is / There are	Há / Aqui está / Aqui estão / São
Family / Parents	Família / Pais
Why	Porque
To say	Dizer
Something	Algo / Alguma coisa
To go	Ir
Ready	Pronto
Soon / quickly	Rápido / Logo
To work	Trabalhar
Who	Quem
To know	Saber

I like to be at my house with my parents
Eu gosto de estar na minha casa com meus pais
I want to know why I need to say something important
Quero saber porque eu precesio dizer alguma coisa importante
I am there with him
Eu estou ali com ele
I am busy, but I need to be ready soon
Eu estou ocupado, mas preciso estar pronto rápido
I like to work
Gosto de trabalhar
Who is there?
Quem está lá?
I want to know if they are here, because I want to go outside
Eu quero saber se eles estão aqui, porque eu quero ir para fora
There are seven dolls
São sete bonecas

How much	Quanto
To bring	Trazer
With me	Comigo
Instead	Em vez
Only	Somente
When	Quando
Lunch	Almoço
Or	Ou
Were	Erão
Without me	Sem eu
Fast / Quickly	Rápido
Slow / Slowly	Devagar
Cold	Frio
Inside	Dentro
To eat	Comer
Hot	Quente
To Drive	Dirigir

How much money do I need to bring with me?
Quanto dinheiro eu preciso trazer comigo?
Instead of this cake, I like that cake
Em vez deste bolo, eu gosto daquele bolo
Only when you can
Somente quando pode
They were without me yesterday
Eles estavam sem mim ontem
I need to drive the car very fast or very slowly
Eu preciso dirigir o carro muito rápido ou muito devagar
It is cold inside the library
Está frio dentro da biblioteca
Yes, I like to eat this hot for my lunch
Sim, eu gosto comer isto quente para meu almoço

To answer	Responder
To fly	Voar
Like (*preposition*)	Como
To travel	Viajar
To learn	Aprender
How	Como
To swim	Nadar
To practice	Praticar
To play	Jogar
To leave	Deixar
Many / A lot	Muito / Muitas
I go to	Eu vou para
First	Primeiro
Time / Times	Vez / Vezes

I need to answer many questions
Eu preciso responder muitas preguntas
I want to fly today
Eu quero voar hoje
I need to learn how to swim at the pool
Eu preciso aprender como nadar na piscina
I want to leave this here for you when I go to travel the world
Eu quero deixar isto para você aqui quando eu vou viajar pelo mundo
Since the first time
Desde a primeira vez
The children are yours
As crianças são tuas

*Pelo mundo literally means "throughout the world."
*With the knowledge you've gained so far, now try to create your own sentences!

Nobody / Anyone	Ninguém
Against	Contra
Us	Nós
To visit	Visitar
Mom / Mother	Mamãe / Mãe
To give	Dar
Which	Qual
To meet	Conhecer
Someone	Alguém
Just	Apenas
To walk	Caminhar/ Andar
Around	Ao redor/em volta
Towards	Para / a traves
Than	Que
Nothing / Anything	Nada

Something is better than nothing
Algo é melhor que nada
I am against him
Eu estou contra ele
We go to visit my family each week
Vamos visitar minha familia cada semana
I need to give you something
Eu preciso te dar algo
Do you want to meet someone?
Você quer conhecer alguém?
I am here on Wednesdays as well
Eu estou aqui às quartas-feiras também
You do this everyday?
Você faz isso todos os dias?
You need to walk around, but not towards the house
Você precisa caminhar em volta, mas nao a traves a casa

Te is a direct and indirect object pronoun, the person who is actually affected by the action that is being carried out. But *te* comes before the verb. For example, "I love you" / *eu te amo* or "to give you" / *te dar.*

I have / I must	Eu tenho / Eu devo
Don't / Doesn't	Não
Friend	Amigo
To borrow	Emprestar
To look like	Parecer
Grandfather	Avô
To want	Querer
To stay	Ficar
To continue	Continuar
Way	Maneira/ Caminho
That's why	Por isso
To show	Mostrar
To prepare	Preperar
I am not going	Eu não vou

Do you want to look like Arnold?
Você quer parecer como Arnold?
I want to borrow this book for my grandfather
Eu quero emprestar este livro do meu avô
I want to drive and to continue on this way to my house
Eu quero dirigir para continuar neste caminho para minha casa
I have a friend, that's why I want to stay in São Paulo
Eu tenho um amigo, por isso eu quero estar aqui em São Paulo
I am not going to see anyone here
Eu não vou ver ninguém aqui
I need to show you how to prepare breakfast
Eu preciso te mostrar como preparar o café da manhã
Why don't you have the book?
Por que você não tem o livro?
That is incorrect, I don't need the car today
Isso é incorreto, eu não preciso do carro hoje
I want to sleep
Eu quero dormir
Where is the airport
Onde é o aeroporto

To remember	Lembrar
Your	(S)(MF)Teu/Tua (P)(M,F)Teus/Tuas
Number	Número
Hour	Hora
Dark / darkness	Escuro / Escuridão
About	Sobre
Grandmother	Avó
Five	Cinco
Minute / Minutes	Minuto / Minutos
More	Mais
To think	Pensar
To do	Fazer
To come	Vir
To hear	Escutar
Last	(M)Último /(F)Última

You need to remember your number
Você precisa lembrar teu número
This is the last hour of darkness
Esta é a última hora da escuridão
I want to come and to hear my grandmother speak Portuguese today
Eu quero vir para escutar a minha avó fala português
I need to think more about this, and what to do
Eu preciso pensar mais sobre isto, e o que fazer
From here until there, it's just five minutes
Daqui até ali, é apenas cinco minutos

To leave	Sair
Again	Outra vez /de novo
Brazil	Brasil
To take	Tomar
To try	Tentar
To rent	Alugar
Without her	Sem ela
We are	Estamos / Somos
To turn off	Apagar
To ask	Pedir
To stop	Parar
Permission	Permissão

He needs to go to rent a house at the beach
Ele precisa ir e alugar uma casa na praia
I want to take the test without her
Eu quero tomar um teste sem ela
We are here a long time
Nós estamos aqui por muito tempo
I need to turn off the lights early
Eu preciso desligar as luzes cedo
We want to stop here
Nós queremos parar aqui
We are from Brazil
Nós somos do Brasil
The same building
O mesmo edifício
I want to ask permission in order to leave
Quero pedir permissão para sair

To open	Abrir
To buy	Comprar
To pay	Pagar
To clean	Limpar
Without	Sem
Sister	Irmã
To hope	Esperar
To live	Viver
Nice to meet you	Prazer em conhecer lo
Name	Nome
Last name	Sobrenome
To return	Regressar
Enough	Suficiente
Door	Porta
Our	Nosso / Nossa
On	Em, sobre

I need to open the door for my sister
Eu preciso abrir a porta para minha irmã
I need to buy something
Eu preciso comprar alguma coisa
I want to meet your sisters
Eu quero conhecer tuas irmãs
Nice to meet you, what is your name and your last name?
Prazer em conhecer lo, qual é o seu nome e, o seu sobrenome?
To hope for the better in the future
Esperar para o melhor no futuro
I want to return from the United States and to live without problems in Brazil
Eu quiero regressar dos Estados Unidos e viver sem problemas no Brasil
Why are you sad right now?
Porque você està triste em neste momento?
Our house is on the mountain
Nossa casa é na montanha

*In Portuguese *on* is *em*, however *on the* is *no/na*. To learn more see page #161.
*This isn't a phrase book! The purpose of this book is solely to provide you with the tools to create your own sentences!

To happen	Ocorrer / acontecer
To order	Ordenar
To drink	Beber
Excuse me	Desculpa
Child	Criança
Woman	Mulher
To begin / To start	Começar
To finish	Terminar
To help	Ajudar
To smoke	Fumar
To love	Amar
To talk / To Speak	Falar

This needs to happen today
Isto precisa acontecer hoje
Excuse me, my child is here as well
Desculpe, minha criança está aqui também
I need to begin soon and to be able to finish at three o'clock in the afternoon
Eu preciso começar rápido e poder para acabar às três horas da tarde
I want to learn how to speak Portuguese
Eu quero apprender como falar Português
I don't want to smoke again
Eu não quero fumar outra vez
I want to help
Eu quero ajudar
I love you
Eu te amo
I see you
Eu te vejo
I need you
Eu preciso de ti

*In Portuguese, "child" is *criança,* "son" is *filho,* and "daughter" is *filha.*

To read	Ler
To write	Escrever
To teach	Ensinar
To close	Fechar
To turn on	Acender / Ligar
To prefer	Preferir
To put	Por / colocar
Less	Menos
Sun	Sol
Month	Mês
I talk / I speak	Eu Falo
Exact	(M)Exato / (F)exata
To choose	Escolher

I need this book to learn how to read and write in Portuguese because I want to teach in Brazil
Eu preciso deste livro para ler e escrever em português porque eu quero ensinar no Brasil
I want to close the door of the house and not to turn on the light
Eu quero fechar a porta da casa e nao apagar as luzes
I prefer to put the gift here
Eu prefiro por o presente aqui
I want to pay less than you for the dinner
Eu quero pagar menos que você para o jantar
I speak with the boy and the girl in Spanish
Eu falo com o menino e a menina em espanhol
There is sun outside today
Há sol lá fora hoje
Is it possible to know the exact date
É possível saber a data exata

*In English, adjectives usually precede the verb. In Portuguese, it's usually the opposite (i.e., "exact date" / *data exata* or "blue car" / *carro azul*).
*With the knowledge you've gained so far, now try to create your own sentences!

To exchange	Trocar / Cambiar
To call	Chamar
Brother	Irmão
Dad	Papai
To sit	Sentar
Together	Juntos
To change	Trocar
Of course	Claro
Welcome	Bemvindo
During	Durante
Years	Anos
Sky	Céu
Up	Encima
Down	Abaixo
Sorry	Desculpe
To follow	Seguir
Him / Her	Lo /La
Big	Grande
New	Novo
Never	Jamais / Nunca

I never want to exchange this money at the bank

Eu nunca quero trocar este dinheiro no banco

I want to call my brother and my dad today

Eu quero chamar meu irmão e meu papai hoje

Of course I can come to the theater, and I want to sit together with you and your sister

Claro eu posso vir a teatro, e eu quero sentar junto contigo e com tua irmã

I need to look below in order to see your new house

Eu preciso olhar em abaixo para ver tua casa nova

I can see the sky from the window

Eu posso ver o céu da janela

I am sorry, but he wants to follow her to the store

Desculpe, mas ele quer segui-la até a loja

*In Portuguese, lo and la are used as direct masculine, feminine, and neuter object pronouns, meaning "him," "her," or "it."
*to see him / vê-lo
*to follow her / sigu-la
The r at the end of the infinitive verb is removed.

To allow	Permitir / deixar
To believe	Crer
Morning	Manhã
Except	Exceto
To promise	Prometer
Good night	Boa noite
To recognize	Reconhecer
People	Pessoas
To move	Mover / Mudar
Far	Distante
Different	Diferente
Man	Homem
To enter	Entrar
To receive	Receber
Throughout	Em todo
Good afternoon	Boa tarde
Through	Atravez
Free	Gratis

I need to allow him to go with us, he is a different man now
Eu preciso deixar ele ir conosco, agora ele é um homem diferente
I believe everything except for this
Eu acredito em tudo exceto isto
I must promise to say good night to my parents each night
Eu preciso prometer de dizer boa noite a meu pais cada noite.
They need to recognize the people from Brazil very quickly
Eles precisam recohnecer as pessoas do Brasil muito rapidamente
I need to move your cat to a different chair
Eu preciso mudar seu gato para uma outra cadeira
They want to enter the competition and receive a free book
Eles querem entrar na competiçao e receber um livro gratis
I see the sun throughout the morning from the kitchen
Eu vejo o sol em toda manhã pelo cozinha
I go into the house but not through the yard
Eu vou por dentro da casa mas não através o jardim

To wish	Desejar
Bad	Mal / mau
To Get	Conseguir
To forget	Esquecer
Everybody	Todos
Although	Embora
To feel	Sentir
Great	Grande
Next	Próximo
To like	Gostar
In front	Em frente
Person	Pessoa
Behind	Atras
Well	Bem
See you soon / Goodbye	Vejo você logo/Tchau
Restaurant	Restaurante
Bathroom	Banheiro

I don't want to wish you anything bad
Eu não quero desejar a você nada de mal
I must forget everybody from my past so I can feel well
Devo esquecer todo mundo do meu pasado para me sentir bem
I am next to the person behind you
Eu estou próximo da pessoa atrás de você
There is a great person in front of me
Aqui esta uma pessoa grande na minha frente
I say goodbye to my friends
Eu digo adeus aos meus amigos
In which part of the restaurant is the bathroom?
Em que parte do restuarante esta o banheiro?
She has to get a car before the next year
Ela tem que conseguir um carro antes do próximo ano
I want to like the house, but it is very small
Eu quero gostar desta casa, mas este muito pequena

To remove	Remover / Retirar
Please	Por favor
Beautiful	(M)Lindo/(F)Linda
To lift	Levantar
Include / Including	Incluir /Incluindo
Belong	Pertencer
To hold	Segurar
To check	Revisar
Small	Pequeno
Real	Real / Verdade
Week	Semana
Size	Tamanho
Even though	Mesmo que
Doesn't	Não
So	Então
Price	Preço

She wants to remove this door please
Por favor, ela quer remover esta porta
This doesn't belong here, I need to check again
Isto não pertencer aqui, preciso revisar outra vez
This week the weather was very beautiful
Esta semana, o tempo estava muito bonito
I need to know which is the real diamond
Eu preciso saber qual é o verdadeiro diamante
We need to check the size of the house
Eu preciso revisar o tamanho desta casa
I want to lift this, so you must hold it high
Eu quero levantar isto, por isso você deve para mantê-lo alto
I can pay this although the price is expensive
Eu posso pagar isto, embora o preço e caro
Including everything, is this price correct?
Incluindo tudo, este preço está correto

BUILDING BRIDGES

In Building Bridges, we take six conjugated verbs that have been selected after studies I have conducted for several months in order to determine which verbs are most commonly conjugated, and which are then automatically followed by an infinitive verb. For example, once you know how to say, "I need," "I want," "I can," and "I like," you will be able to connect words and say almost anything you want more correctly and understandably. The following three pages contain these six conjugated verbs in first, second, third, fourth, and fifth person, as well as some sample sentences. Please master the entire program up until *here* prior to venturing onto this section.

I want	Quero
I need	Preciso
I can	Posso
I like	Gosto
I go	Vou
I have / I must	Tenho

I want to go to my house
Eu quero ir a minha casa
I can go with you to the bus station
Eu posso ir contigo para a estação de ônibus
I need to walk outside the museum
Eu preciso caminhar fora deste museu
I like to eat oranges
Eu gosto de comer laranjas
I am going to teach a class
Eu vou ensinar uma classe
I have to speak to my teacher
Tenho que falar com meu professor

*In Portuguese similar to Spanish, "I have", *tenho* when followed by a verb you must always place a *que*, proceeding the *tenho*, or *ter* (infinitive form of to have). I have to speak, *tenho que falar*. To learn more please see page #160.

Please master every single page up until here prior to attempting the following two pages!

You want / do you want	Você quer
He wants / does he want	Ele quer
She wants / does she want	Ela quer
We want / do we want	Nós queremos
They want / do they want	Eles/elas querem
You (plural) want	Vocês querem

You need / do you need	Você precisa
He needs / does he need	Ele precisa
She needs / does she need	Ela precisa
We want / do we want	Nós precisamos
They need / do they need	Eles/elas precisam
You (plural) need	Vocês precisam

You can / can you	Você pode
He can / can he	Ele pode
She can / can she	Ela pode
We can / can we	Nós podemos
They can / can they	Eles/elas Podem
You (plural) can	Vocês podem

You like / do you like	Você gosta
He likes / does he like	Ele gosta
She like / does she like	Ela gosta
We like / do we like	Nós gostamos
They like / do they like	Eles/elas gostam
You (plural) like	Vocês gostam

You go / do you go	Você vai
He goes / does he go	Ele vai
She goes / does she go	Ela vai
We go / do we go	Nós vamos
They go / do they go	Eles/elas vão
You (plural) go	Vocês vão

You have / do you have	Você tem
He has / does he have	Ele tem
She has / does she have	Ela tem
We have / do we have	Nós temos
They have / do they have	Eles/elas têm
You (plural) have	Vocês têm

Do you want to go?
Você quer ir?
Does he want to fly?
Ele quer voar?
We want to swim
Queremos nadar
Do they want to run?
Querem correr
Do you need to clean?
Você precisa limpar?
She needs to sing a song
Ela precisa cantar um canção
We need to travel
Precisamos viajar
They don't need to fight
Eles não precisam lutar
You (plural) need to see
Vocês precisam ver
Can you hear me?
Pode me escuctar?
He can dance very well
Pode dançar muito bem
We can go out tonight
Podemos sair esta noite
They can break the wood
Podem quebrar a madera
Do you like to eat here?
Gosta de comer aqui?

He likes to spend time here
Gosta de passar tempo aqui
We like to fix the house
Gostamos de arrumar a casa
They like to cook
Eles gostam de cozinhar
You (plural) like my house
Vocês gostam da minha casa
Do you go to school today?
Você vai à escola hoje
He goes fishing
Ele vai pescar
We are going to relax
Vamos relaxar
They go to watch a film
Eles vão ver um filme
Do you have money?
Você tem dinheiro?
She has to look outside
Ela tem que olhar para fora
We have to sign our names
Temos que assinar os nossos nomes
They have to send the letter
Eles tem que mandar/enviar a carta
You (plural) have to order
Vocês tem que ordinar

*Whenever refering to a group in which you have all female individuals, you refer to that group as ELAS. Mixed male and female individuals refer to them as ELES.

BASIC GRAMMATICAL REQUIREMENTS OF THE PORTUGUESE LANGUAGE WHICH YOU WILL ENCOUNTER IN THIS PROGRAM

Feminine and Masculine & Plural and Singular

In the Portuguese language, there are plural and singular words, as well as masculine and feminine words. For example, the article "the," for Portuguese words ending with an a, e, and i, will usually be deemed to be feminine, the article will usually be a. Nouns ending with an o will generally be masculine, and the article will usually be o. The article "the" in plural form is os for the masculine form, and as for the feminine form. "The boy" is o (the) menino (boy). "The girl" is a menina, "the boys" is os meninos, and "the girls" is as meninas.

The conjugation of the article "a" (um and uma) is determined by masculine and feminine form: "a car" / um carro or "a house" / uma casa.

The conjugation for "this" (esta, este, estes, and estas) and "that" (esse, essa, esses, and essas). This, este is masculine, este livro ("this book"). Feminine is esta, for example, esta casa ("this house"). Estes livros ("these books") and estas casas ("these houses") are the plural forms. "That," esse, is masculine, esse livro ("that book"). Feminine is essa, essa cadeira ("that chair"). In plural, that is esses livros (these books) and essas cadeiras ("these chairs").

"Of" has singular and plural forms as well: do and dos.

Isso and isto are neuter pronouns, meaning they don't have a gender. They usually refer to an idea or an unknown object that isn't specifically named. For example, "that" is isto.

isto é / "that is", por isso / "because of that"

"This" is isto. Isto esta bom / "this is good", o que é isto? / "what is this?"

In regards to "my," singular and plural form exists as well as feminine and masculine. Meu is masculine, minha is feminine, meus is masculine plural, and minhas is feminine plural. "my chair" / minha cadeira, "my chairs" / minhas cadeiras, "my money" / meu dinheiro, "my papers" / meus papéis

With regard to "your," teu (masculine) and tua (feminine), plural teus and tuas. Example in masculine and feminine singular: teu carro / "your car", your house / "tua casa". The plural teus carros and tuas casas.

"Of" has singular and plural forms as well: do and dos.

Temporary and Permanent

The different forms of "is" are é and está. When referring to a permanent condition, for example, "she is a girl" / ela é uma menina, you use é. For temporary positions, "the girl is doing well today" / a menina está muito bem hoje, you use está.

"You are" / "are you" could mean estas, and it could also mean tu eres. An example of temporary position is "How are you today?" / "Como você está?" as well as "you are here" / está aqui.

Another example of permanent position is "are you Mexican?" / você é Mexicano? in addition to "You are a man!" / você é um homem!

* **"I am"—estou and eu sou.** Eu sou refers to a permanent condition: "I am Italian" / eu sou Italiano. Temporary condition would be "I am at the mall" / estou no mall.

* **"We are"—somos (permanent) and estamos (temporary).** Nós somos Peruanos / "we are Peruvian" and nos estamos no parque / "we are at the park."

* **"Are"—são (permanent) and estão (temporary).** Eles são Chilenos / "they **are** Chileans" and eles estão no carro / "they are in the car."

Synonyms and Antonyms

There are three ways of describing time.

Vez / vezes—"first time" / primeira vez or "three times" / três vezes

Tempo—"during the time of the dinosaurs" /durante o tempo dos dinossauros

Hora—"What time is it?" / Que hora são?

Que has four definitions.

"What"—O que é isso? / "What is this?"

"Than"—Eu estou melhor que você / "I am better than you"

"That"—"I want to say that I am near the house" / eu quero dizer que estou perto de casa

"I must" / "I have to"—Tenho que. The verb ter, "to have," whether it's in conjugated or infinitive form, if it's followed by another verb, then que must always follow.

For example:

* I have to swim now, tenho que nadar agora.

Deixar has two definitions.

"To leave"—Eu quero deixar isto aqui / "I want to leave this here." Deixar is "to leave" something, but when saying "to leave" as in "going," it's sair, for example, "I want to leave now" / quero sair agora.

"To allow"—Deixar could also mean to "allow."

There are two ways of describing "so."

"So"—então. Using it to replace "then." "So I need to know." / Então preciso saber.

"So"—tão. Isso é tão distante. / "This is so far."

Verb Conjugation in First Person

"I" / Eu before a conjugated verb isn't required. For example, Eu preciso saber a data / "I need to know the date" can be said Preciso saber a data, because preciso already means "I need," in conjugated form. Although saying Eu isn't incorrect! The same can also be said with você / tu; ele / ela; nos; eles / elas, in which they aren't required to be placed prior to the conjugated verb, but if they are, then it isn't wrong.

Connecting words

In Portuguese, certain words can connect, creating one syllable. For example, the article*the* , in masculine form **o**, feminine form **a**

In(em)+the(o)=no, in the car, **no** carro
em+a=na, in the house, **na** casa
In(em) and *this(essa),* **em+essa; nessa;** In this house, **nessa** casa
In this car; **em+esse; nesse** carro
em+este = **neste; neste** carro
em+esta = **nesta** casa
In(em) his(ele) = **nele;** in his car, **nele** carro
In(em) her(ela) = **nela;** in her house, **nela** casa
Our house, **Nossa** casa / *Our car,* **Nosso** carro

His car, **de+ele** = carro **dele** / her car, carro **dela**
Their car, carro **deles** / (fem) their car / carro **delas**

Of and*this* can connect as well creating one syllable,
de+isso; I need this, eu preciso **disso**
de+esse; from this side, **desse** lado
de+esses; these men, **desses** homes
de+essas; these women, **dessas** mulheres
de+isso = **disto**
de+aqui = **daqui**
de+onde = **donde**
de+outro = **doutro**

OTHER USEFUL TOOLS FOR
THE PORTUGUESE LANGUAGE

Reading and Pronunciation

Ã can be pronounced as either "uh" or "un" however it must be nasalized. *Ção* pronounced as sun-o.

Ç is pronounced like "s," whenever it precedes a, o, or u. *Criança* is pronounced as "criansa."

D is pronounced as "dj" whenever preceding an i or an e. *Tarde* is pronounced as "tardje." *Dia* is pronounced as "gia."

H is silent except when followed by an n.

L is pronounced as "ee-oo" whenever it follows an a or i. *Brasil* is pronounced as "Bra-zee-oo."

M is pronounced as a soft "m" whenever it's the last letter of a word. One trick for pronunciation is saying it without closing your lips.

R is pronounced as an "h" if it's the first letter of the word. *Roberto* is "Hoberto." Whenever r is the last letter of a word, then it's pronounced very softly.

S is pronounced like a "z" whenever it's between vowels or when it's at the end of the word. *Português* is pronounced as "Portuguêz."

T is pronounced as "tchi" whenever preceding an e or an i. *Contigo* is pronounced as "contchigo."

U is pronounced like "oo."

W is pronounced like a "v." *William* is pronounced as "Villiam."

X is usually pronounced as "sh" whenever preceding a vowel. *Deixar* is pronounced as "deis har." Whenever preceding a consonant, X is usually pronounced as "s." *Exterior* is pronounced as "esterior." When between vowels, X is usually pronounced as "ks." *Fixo* is "fikso." For words that begin in ex or hex, followed by a vowel, the x is pronounced like a z. *Hexágono* is "hezágono." But in Portuguese, x is one of those letters where there are no set rules for its pronunciation!

Z is pronounced as a "ss" whenever it's at the end of a word. *Alvarez* is pronounced as "Alvaress."

Diphthongs

ai - is pronounced like the ie in pie

ão - is pronounced like the ow in clown

au - is pronounced like the ow in now

ei - is pronounced like the ay in pay

eu - is pronounced as ay-oo like the ay in hay + the oo in boot

ho - is pronounced like a soft o

ia - is pronounced ee-ah like the ee in feet + the a in father

ie - is pronounced like the e in yes

io - is pronounced ee-oh

iu - is pronounced ee-oo like the ee in meet + the oo in loot

oi - is pronounced "closed" like the oy in toy

ou - is pronounced like the ow in glow

õ - is pronounced nasalized

ua - is pronounced like the oo-ah in watch minus the w sound

ue - is pronounced oo-eh like the oo in loot and the ay in day

ui - is pronounced like oo-ee the oo in loot and the ee in meet

uo - is pronounced like the uo in quota

Diagraphs

lh - is pronounced like lli in alligator

nh - is pronounced like ni in minion; or like mañana in Spanish

rr - pronounced like h, terra will be pronounced teh-ha

Accents

Á - is pronounced like the *y* in *fly*, when at the end of the word pronounced like *a* in *another*

À - is pronounced like the *a* in *another*

Â - is pronounced like a long *a*

Ó - is pronounced like *oy*

É - is pronounced like the *a* in *many*

Ê - pronounced like a long *e*

Ì - is pronounced like the *e* in *embrace*

Ó - is pronounced *oy*, when last letter of word like *u* in *jump*

Ô - is pronounced like a long *o*

Ú and **Û** - pronounced like the *oo* in *loot*

Days of the Week

Sunday	Domingo
Monday	Segunda-feira
Tuesday	Terça-feira
Wednesday	Quarta-feira
Thursday	Quinta-feira
Friday	Sexta-feira
Saturday	Sábado

Seasons

Spring	Primavera
Summer	Verão
Autumn	Outono
Winter	Inverno

Cardinal Directions

North	Norte
South	Sul
East	Leste
West	Oeste

Colors

Black	Preto
White	Branco
Gray	Cinza
Red	Vermelho
Blue	Azul
Yellow	Amarelo
Green	Verde
Orange	Laranja
Purple	Roxo
Brown	Marrom

Numbers

One	Um
Two	Dois
Three	Três
Four	Quatro
Five	Cinco
Six	Sies
Seven	Sete
Eight	Oito
Nine	Nove
Ten	Dez

CONGRATULATIONS, NOW YOU ARE ON YOUR OWN!

If you merely absorb the required three hundred and fifty words in this book, you will then have acquired the basis to become conversational in these languages! After memorizing these three hundred and fifty words, this conversational foundational basis that you have just gained will trigger your ability to make improvements in conversational fluency at an amazing speed! However, in order to engage in quick and easy conversational communication, you need a special type of basics, and this book will provide you with just that.

Unlike the foreign language learning systems presently used in schools and universities, along with books and programs that are available on the market today, that focus on *everything* but being conversational, *this* method's sole focus is on becoming conversational in the language as well as any other language. Once you have successfully mastered the required words in this book, there are two techniques that if combined with these essential words, can further enhance your skills and will result in you improving your proficiency tenfold. *However*, these two techniques will only succeed *if* you have completely and successfully absorbed the three hundred and fifty words. *After* you establish the basis for fluent communications by memorizing these words, you can enhance your conversational abilities even more if you use the following two techniques.

The first step is to attend a language class, in the language of your desire, that will enable you to sharpen your grammar. You will gain additional vocabulary and learn past and present tenses, and if you apply these skills that you learn in the class, together with the three hundred and fifty words that you have previously memorized, you will be improving your conversational skills tenfold. You will notice that, conversationally, you will succeed at a much higher rate than any of your classmates. A simple second technique is to choose subtitles in that language of your choosing while watching a movie. If you have successfully mastered and grasped these three hundred and fifty words, then the combination of the two—those words along with the subtitles—will aid you considerably in putting all the grammar into perspective, and again, conversationally, you will improve tenfold.

Once you have established a basis of quick and easy conversation in that language with those words that you just attained, every additional word or grammar rule you pick up from there on will be gravy. And these additional words or grammar rules can be combined with the three hundred and fifty words, enriching your conversational abilities even more. Basically, after the research and studies I've conducted with my method over the years, I came to the conclusion that in order to become conversational, you first must learn the words and then learn the grammar.

These languages are compatible with the mirror translation technique. Likewise, with this language, you can use this mirror translation technique in order to become conversational, enabling you to communicate even more effortlessly. Mirror translation is the method of translating a phrase or sentence, word for word from English into the foreign language, by using these imperative words that you have acquired through this program (such as the sentences I used in this book). Latin languages, Middle Eastern languages, and Slavic languages, along with a few others, are also compatible with the mirror translation technique. Though you won't be speaking perfectly proper and precise in the language, you will still be fully understood and, conversation-wise, be able to get by just fine.

CONCLUSION

Congratulations! You have completed all the tools needed to master the Spanish, French, Italian, and Portuguese language, and I hope that this has been a valuable learning experience. Now you have sufficient communication skills to be confident enough to embark on a visit to Europe or South America, impress your friends, and boost your resume so good luck.

This program is available in other languages as well, and it is my fervent hope that my language learning programs will be used for good, enabling people from all corners of the globe and from all cultures and religions to be able to communicate harmoniously. After memorizing the required three hundred and fifty words, please perform a daily five-minute exercise by creating sentences in your head using these words. This simple exercise will help you grasp conversational communications even more effectively. Also, once you memorize the vocabulary on each page, follow it by using a notecard to cover the words you have just memorized and test yourself and follow that by going back and using this same notecard technique on the pages you studied during the previous days. This repetition technique will assist you in mastering these words in order to provide you with the tools to create your own sentences.

Every day, use this notecard technique on the words that you have just studied.

Everything in life has a catch. The catch here is just consistency. If you just open the book, and after the first few pages of studying the program, you put it down, then you will not gain anything. However, if you consistently dedicate a half hour daily to studying, as well as reviewing what you have learned from previous days, then you will quickly realize why this method is the most effective technique ever created to become conversational in a foreign language. My technique works! For anyone who doubts this technique, all I can say is that it has worked for me and hundreds of others.

Note from the Author

Thank you for your interest in my work. I encourage you to share your overall experience of this book by posting a review. Your review can make a difference! Please feel free to describe how you benefited from my method or provide creative feedback on how I can improve this program. I am constantly seeking ways to enhance the quality of this product, based on personal testimonials and suggestions from individuals like you.
Thanks and best of luck,
Yatir Nitzany

CPSIA information can be obtained
at www.ICGtesting.com
Printed in the USA
LVHW082038190620
658572LV00007B/2018